RUSSIAИ cooking

ROBIN HOWE

Foreword by **Jennifer Paterson**

ANDRE DEUTSCH

First published in Great Britain in 1964 by André Deutsch Ltd

This edition first published in 1998 by André Deutsch Ltd
76 Dean Street
London W1V 5HA

www.vci.co.uk

André Deutsch is a VCI plc company

1 3 5 7 9 10 8 6 4 2

Printed and bound in Great Britain by St Edmundsbury Press, Suffolk

A catalogue record for this book is available from the British Library

ISBN 0 23399 472 6

Design by Kee Scott Associates

Contents

RUSSIAN cooking

Foreword

I am delighted that this fascinating book is being revived. I had never heard of it and thought Robin Howe was a man, which she obviously was not – she had a nice husband who was most accommodating in his role of chief taster. There are very few Russian cookbooks about and this is a magnificent collection of receipts from every region of Russia, including treasured family ones from White Russian friends who have preserved their old ways, and others from modern Russian contacts Robin met in her world wide travels. She writes most engagingly, with both joy and wit. Excellent new ideas are to be gleaned from the Zakuski (Hors d'Oeuvre) section to liven up the constant M & S canapes so often found at drinks parties. A detailed description of how to make Kulich (Easter Cake) would deter all but the most intrepid of cooks. It is a whole day's work and requires real strength for kneading. It contains fifteen egg yolks, amongst other things, and the whole thing can be ruined by a draught of air or a slammed door; very frightening but a triumph if successful.

Sauces seem to be mostly flavoured bechamels, and of course a great deal of sour cream and curd cheese are used, let alone Kumys – fermented mare's milk – which is still impossible to achieve in this country as we don't have the right culture. Nowadays you can probably find all the necessary ingredients here. Read, enjoy, and cook.

Introduction

I think the difference between old style Russian cooking and the present is best illustrated by two paragraphs of culinary observation. The first is taken from that enchanting book, *Oblomov* by Ivan Goncharov.

'Food was the first and foremost interest in life at Oblomovka. What calves were fattened there for feast-days! What birds were bred! Turkeys and chickens intended for name days and other solemn occasions were fed on nuts; geese were deprived of exercise and forced to hang motionless in a bag for a few days before the feast so that they could get coated with fat. What stores of jams, pickles, biscuits there were! What meads, what *kvasses* were brewed, what pies were baked at Oblomovka!

'...the women travelled several times from the storeroom to the kitchen with a double quantity of eggs and flour; there were more shrieks and bloodshed than usual in the poultry-yard. A tremendous pie was baked, which was served to the family for two days in succession...'

Contrast this with the following paragraph which appeared in an article entitled, 'Kitchen of a Thousand Housewives', in *The Soviet Woman*.

'Women carrying dinner pans and market bags walked on the sunny side of the street and we did not have to look up the address of the home service kitchen in our note-books. As we followed them we entered a room fitted with white tiles. There were smells of sweetmeats, cake, roast-meat and borsch in the air.

'The sun's rays which streamed in through the broad windows flooded the counter, sparkling on the jellied foods, and the fluffy sponge cake and pies and penetrating the pile of chips. Everything looked very nice and wholesome and we were not a bit surprised to find so many buyers. The door leading from the kitchen was frequently pushed open by an employee in a white overall carrying huge plates of steaming beetroot, boiled potatoes and carrots. There was a brisk sale of varieties of meat and vegetables for borsch, ressolnik [soup with pickled cucumbers] and pea soup.'

In this particular kitchen it was reported they sold daily '200 cooked dinners, 450 soup sets, 300kg [660lb] of boiled vegetables, 1,500 stuffed cabbage rolls and vegetable cutlets.'

The prepared dinners and 'soup sets' cost on an average 5 to 10 per cent more than a meal prepared at home but I am assured that it is the ambition of the Russian family to be able to buy more and more of the cooked meals in order 'to relieve mother of the extra burden of cooking' when she returns from factory, office or other place of work to which, as a true Russian citizen, she goes every day.

RUSSIAN cooking

In the old Russia those who cooked were passionately attached to their metiér and a cordon bleu was indeed a cordon bleu. Today I am assured that cooks are on the 'suspect list', an assertion I find hard to believe. However, it is enough to say that such an assertion is made to understand the official reaction to the delights of cooking.

It is not easy for the Russian cook to be interested in cooking. She seldom enjoys the privilege and pleasure of her own kitchen. This essential room she may share not with one neighbour, but with several. Enthusiastic Russian apologists explain the housing shortage as being the direct result of the wartime scorched earth policy, and they may well be right, just as in Leningrad they attribute their very large appetites to the starvation they suffered during the siege of this city.

However, despite the cooking troubles of the big cities in what might be termed 'Western' Russia, still in the Ukraine and in the Caucasian areas there is a good deal of home cooking, mostly done by the older generation of women with long memories. The Ukrainians and the Caucasians prided themselves, and still do, on being the finest cooks in Russia.

Russian bakeries are excellent; so are the delicatessen stores. There are several varieties of bread, white and soft as well as a black bread which is almost as rich and sweet as a fruit cake. In the Asiatic States flat, unleavened bread is eaten, as it is in most parts of the Near and Far East. Called nan, it is extremely good when fresh.

Russian meals and meal times differ vastly from the British pattern. Those of us addicted to a breakfast of porridge, eggs and bacon would cry with horror at the sight of a Russian consuming chunks of good black bread, cheese or salami; or of a man in an hotel consuming vast quantities of caviar and raw onion in the grey light of dawn.

A Russian lunch is roughly the same time as our own, noon, as it is often the main meal of the day. Dinner can be eaten almost any time in the evening, from five o'clock to midnight, although a favourite time for dinner is around ten o'clock after a long session of *zakuski* eating.

This dinner might sometimes consist simply of a continuation of the *zakuski* eating, or simply be a snack meal with a soup course.

As far as the Russian takes tea in our sense of the word, this can be an enormous meal, with jam and cakes, bread and biscuits, chocolates and cognac. On special occasions, in fact, it is possible to consume a five course tea, if taking a traditional tea.

In many parts of the former Soviet Union the ancient custom of 'breaking bread' is still observed, presenting a guest who is entering the house for the

Introduction

first time with a small loaf of bread, topped with salt, and lying in a clean embroidered napkin. This ceremony is symbolic of well-being and fertility, the best of treasures the earth can offer man for his labours.

Menu's differ widely in the states that make up the former Soviet Union. In Siberia a hostess likes to offer *pelmeni* (similar to Italian ravioli) cooked in soup or in a well-flavoured stock. In the Caucasus she offers shashlik or a lentil soup; while the Baltic Republics prefer small dumplings, an inheritance from their German or Baltic baron influences. The Moldavians have a preference for aubergine and small patties, while the Karelians have a speciality of fish cooked in milk, simple but satisfying. In the Central Asian Republics they like heavily spiced foods, pilaus, or *plovs*, which they eat with their fingers, saying with scorn, 'In Russia they eat food with forks because their hands are dirty,' a point of view shared by many Indians who feel that they know their hands are clean, but what does one know of a silver fork? Women, curiously enough, are not expected to enjoy over-spiced or hot food, which, for visiting women tourists, is probably on the whole quite a good thing.

Some Russian recipes are of obscure origin, but there are some direct influences which can be traced. Peter the Great brought in the Germans, who together with the Baltic barons, brought with them their sauerkraut, schnitzel and sausages; the Italians drifted in with noodles, salami and macaroni; the French brought their more subtle influences in cooking. Lack of refrigeration and transport made sour cream or *smetana* popular; the peasants with their cabbage, *kasha* and black bread introduced a strong plebeian note, and out of this Russian cooking emerged, developed and became one of the popular kitchens of the world.

The recipes in this book have come, in the main, from emigré Russian sources, although they have been checked against present day Russian cooking books, of which there are not many.

The cook of a friend of mine in Moscow, kindly marked in pencil (a red one, which was probably unconscious symbolism) the recipes she herself liked to prepare and which, she said, most foreigners preferred her to make and she had been cooking for various diplomatic missions for many years.

I think I am fair in saying that all the ingredients mentioned in this book are obtainable in London and elsewhere in Britain. Many are even more easily obtained in the country than in towns.

Most of the dishes are for 4 to 6 people, although on the whole I am not fond of stressing how much is for how many, since, like figures, appetites vary enormously.

RUSSIAN cooking

Hors d'Oeuvre
Zakuski

These are Russian Hors d'Oeuvre, the parent of all Hors d'Oeuvre.

The old *zakuski* spreads must have been fabulous, to judge by the descriptions of one's Russian friends and from the reading of Russian books. Countless bowls and dishes of countless varieties of food, all washed down by equally countless glasses of liquor, not always vodka, although vodka and *zakuski* go together.

I remember when I was very young and living in Berlin, many years before the last war, the city boasted several Russian restaurants and a large Russian emigré colony. These restaurants seemed to be always full of sad and very soulful-looking Russians. It was with one of these 'soulful' Russians that I had my first taste of Russian *zakuski*. The table appeared to me to be spread generously; but my host, as he reminisced, said, 'Ah, my dear, if you think this table is richly spread you should have seen the tables of my family and friends in St Petersburg. I remember at Eastertime my father and uncles would go from house to house, drinking and sampling the *zakuski*, for we do not drink without eating. What giants they were, gormandizing giants... What is this?' He answered his own question. 'A peasant's meal.' As I nibbled I thought what a lucky peasant.

Today one could easily offer a *zakuski* spread as a main meal. It makes for easy serving, especially when one realizes that to be traditional one must eat standing up, although there is no absolute need to stand up all the evening, I suppose. Much of the *zakuski* spread can be bought ready for the table; much made with east at home. Any or all of the following dishes could be offered. Vodka, any form of schnaps, Danzig brandy (if available) and any of the cognacs could be served.

Caviar, all varieties.
Fish in aspic.
All kinds of pickled and soused fish.
Kidneys and liver cooked in various ways.
Sardines, anchovies and smelts.
Stuffed green peppers and tomatoes, hot or cold.
Olives, black and green.
Blinis, served hot, wrapped in a napkin.

Hors d'Oeuvre
Zakuski

All kinds of mushroom dishes, cooked, marinated, salted, etc.
Pickled cucumbers and other pickled vegetables.
Cheese tartlets.
Sausages, heavily laced with garlic or in a sauce.
Salted herrings, plain or made into pies, etc.
Curd cheese in every conceivable way of serving it.
All kinds of smoked fish, in particular smoked salmon.
Any of the large or small Russian pies (see pages 177–81)
Cooked meat cut into thin slices, especially in aspic.
'Baskets' filled with salad, caviar or other delicacies.
Eggs, hard-boiled, poached, baked, scrambled, etc.
Chicken liver pâté.
Salads of all kinds.
Brawns, again of all kinds, especially from pork.
Sauces, again all varieties, especially horseradish.

Among the sandwiches, or canapés could be listed:

Fried ham and fried chopped onion.
Fried sausages and fried bacon.
Boiled and sliced ham, smeared generously with mustard.
Boiled, sliced ham with chopped, fried tomatoes, etc.

RUSSIAN cooking

Caviar

Ikra

It had not occurred to me, before preparing this book, that caviar was not the Russian name for this, the finest of all their *zakuski* dishes. I for one, among many other gourmets, would at any time happily forgo more gastronomic pleasures, for a portion of this delicious product from the regal sturgeon. I like to think that I could never have too much of it, and remember one period in my life when I ate caviar every day at noon for ten days, and the wonderful evening when my husband and I slowly ate a pound of caviar between us ... accompanied by a bottle of champagne, and the scent of the magnolia tree at the bottom of the garden. Below us lay the Bosphorus with its fairy steamers plying to and fro. We ate slowly and happily. It is difficult with such memories to appreciate those exasperated British soldiers stationed on the Black Sea during one of the wars, who complained with characteristic jocularity, 'We'd 'ad enuff of this 'ere black fish jam.'

Caviar comes from the salted roe of the sturgeon; the finest of all from the sterlet. The latter, in the days of the tsars, was reserved for the royal tables. Accurately, only sturgeon eggs should be called caviar. The so called 'red' caviar, although delicious in its own way, is prepared from the eggs of salmon, and scorned by true caviar devotees as a feeble substitute for the genuine article. However, this type of 'caviar' does have an excellent and completely distinctive flavour and, oddly, when used as a flavouring in bland fish dishes, it surpasses the black.

Caviar in Russia is certainly less expensive than in most countries, but even so it is not sold at what might be called 'give away' prices.

The name 'fresh caviar' applies to the choice, firm, but not too ripe eggs of the three main strugeon species, yielding roes of three sizes. But one learns with experience that all which glistens black and oily is not true caviar. The eggs of the cod, the catfish, the whiting, shad and mullet are also pressed, processed and dyed to give the dark colour, which should, but does not always, denote true caviar. However, the connoisseur can tell by the taste what he is eatin and the real expert can tell even in which waters the sturgeon was caught.

Caviar at its best is eaten *au naturel*, that is, on brown or white bread, without butter. The caviar itself should be far and oily enough not to require the addition of any other fat. Neither should it require the addition of such embellishments as lemon juice, chopped hard-boiled eggs, chopped onions or onion juice. However, some caviar, being more salted than others, can take a little lemon juice, and even in Russia caviar is often served with tiny shreds of thin spring onions. *Malosso*, which in Russia means 'little salt', is a term applied to any caviar which is mildly salted, and for many this is the preferred kind.

Once a jar of caviar has been opened it will quickly lose its freshness. It should not be kept too long. If, however, you must keep caviar for a short time, recover the container and lie it on its side to allow the oil to seep through the grains. If keeping for a few days, turn it from time to time. After dipping into the jar, flatten the disturbed grains with the blade of a knife, so there are no holes for the juice to run through. This drains off the moisture from the remaining grains.

Red caviar is also eaten a great deal in Russia, and with evident enjoyment, but it is not regarded as caviar, rather as a pleasant or delicate item of eating for hot days.

Sturgeon caviar and caviar from the salmon are often served together; the black or grey sturgeon caviar in small bowls (or large bowls) and the sliced, pressed salmon caviar in oval-shaped dishes. Chopped spring onions are served separately, also wedges of lemon. A bowl of caviar and a large raw onion is considered a fine breakfast by those who can afford luxuries.

The following are descriptions of the main caviar types:

Beluga

This is a large grained caviar coming from the sturgeon of the same name. It is for the gourmet and those 'who eat with their eyes'. The grains are black, medium-black and fine grey. There is also a 'golden caviar' which every caviar connoisseur hopes to find one day, even if only to taste the most minute portion.

Osetr

A caviar which has the distinction (perhaps to many a doubtful distinction) of having been the favourite of Nikita Khrushchev. It comes from a smaller sturgeon than the beluga, which can weigh up to 900kg (2000lb) and more. The Osetr achieves only a mere 320kg (700lb).

RUSSIAN cooking

Sevruga

A species of sturgeon yielding the smallest grained caviar, which is much appreciated by caviar fanciers.

Payasnaya

A coarsely grained, lightly packed black caviar, heavily salted and produced from genuine grains but from those which have been damaged in the sieving process, or are premature. Cheaper than the whole grain caviar, it is a favourite among experts, especially Russians, many of whom prefer this type of caviar to any other. It is largely prepared in Astrakhan for export and packed in barrels.

Aubergine Caviar (Poor Man's Caviar)

Baklazhannaya Ikra

This type of 'caviar' is to be found in almost all of those countries where the aubergine is as popular as the cabbage is in Britain.

Generally the aubergines are cooked over charcoal until their skins are slightly burnt and peel easily. This gives the 'caviar' a slightly burnt flavour. However, where it is not easy to burn the skins over charcoal, try roasting them in a hot oven. Peel and coarsely chop up the flesh.

2 fairly large aubergines (treated as above)	*1 peeled, seeded and chopped tomato*
1 medium grated onion	*Salt and pepper*
Green pepper to taste (capsicum)	*Olive oil*

Do not use more than half a medium-sized pepper. Remove the pith and seeds and chop the rest very finely. (Some cooks put the pepper into cold water to remove any bitterness, but this is a matter for personal preference.)

Heat a small quantity of olive oil, add the onion and fry this until it becomes pink-brown. Add the tomato, the chopped pepper, salt and pepper and cook gently until the mixture is very soft. Rub this through a sieve. Mash the aubergine until it is smooth. Mix it with the remaining ingredients and, when completely blended, put the mixture into a dish and leave until it is cold.

Serve as a salad, with chunks of dark bread to be used as a scoop.

Another method is to chop and mash the aubergine as above, mix it with salt and pepper, some finely chopped dill and enough olive oil and lemon juice to make a smooth consistency, rather like a very thick mayonnaise.

Aubergine with a Sour Cream Sauce

Baklazhany V Smyetannom Sousye

1 large aubergine	25g (1oz) plain flour
Oil for deep frying	300ml (1/2 pint) sour cream
40g (11/2oz) butter	Fresh single cream

Peel the aubergine and cut it into thick slices. Sprinkle with salt and leave long enough for the liquid content to ooze out. Wipe the slices dry. (If in a hurry, ignore this advice.) Heat the oil and fry the aubergine slices on both sides until golden brown and crisp.

Take the aubergine from the pan and drain. Melt the butter in a small saucepan and stir in the flour. Take the pan off the stove and gradually add the sour cream. Return the pan to the stove and gradually reheat. Slowly stir in 1 or 2 tablespoons of fresh cream, to loosen the sauce.

Arrange the slices of aubergine in individual plates. Add the cream, covering each slice of aubergine. Put the plates for a few moments under the grill to lightly brown the top of the sauce.

Yoghurt may be used instead of sour cream in the same manner.

Stuffed Aubergine

Baklazhany Farshirovannyye

700g (11/2lb) aubergine (about 2 large ones)	Butter or oil for frying
1 tablespoon chopped button mushrooms	Breadcrumbs

Peel the aubergines, cut into halves, remove part of the inside, sprinkle the shells with salt and leave for 30 minutes. (This causes the surplus liquid to ooze out.) Wipe dry, roll in plain flour and very lightly fry. Put into a shallow baking dish.

Chop up the removed flesh and mix with the mushrooms. Add salt and pepper and crushed garlic (all to taste). Pack this mixture into the aubergine shells, sprinkle with breadcrumbs and bake at 190°C/375°F/Gas 5 until the aubergines are soft.

It is hard to give the exact quantities of oil or butter for frying. Aubergines usually take a lot of fat, and oil is probably better as a frying medium in this case. The quantity of mushrooms may be doubled, or field mushrooms substituted.

Cucumber in Sour Cream

Ogurtsy V Smyetanye

The quantities can only be approximate since the size of cucumbers can vary.

1 fresh cucumber, medium size	1/2 tablespoon wine vinegar
300ml (1/2 pint) sour cream, or yoghurt	Salt and pepper to taste
	Chopped fresh dill or parsley

Peel the cucumber and either cut it into slices or dice (I prefer to dice). Sprinkle with salt and pepper. Mix the vinegar into the sour cream or yoghurt and pour this over the cucumber. Sprinkle with chopped dill or parsley. Serve ice-cold.

Serve with cold meat dishes. The best kind of cucumbers for this dish are the small, rather juicy variety. In any case, the smaller and younger the better.

Stuffed Peppers (Capsicum)

Pyeryets, Farshirovannyi Myasom

6 large peppers	Salt and pepper
50g (2oz) basmati rice	Chopped fresh dill or parsley
100–175g (4–6oz) beef or lamb	25g (1oz) butter
1 large chopped onion	Sour cream or tomato sauce
Vegetable stock	(see pages 196–7)

Hors d'Oeuvre
Zakuski

Choose peppers which are of equal size and will 'sit' well when stuffed. They should be almost square at the bottom. Cook the rice in rapidly boiling water for no more than 10 minutes. Drain and put aside until needed. Drop the peppers into boiling water and leave for 3 minutes. Drain and, as soon as you can handle them, cut the tops of neatly and scoop out the seeds. Put the meat through a mincer (the original recipe says twice, but once is sufficient). Melt the butter and lightly fry the onion.

Mix the rice, onion, minced meat and a little stock, only enough to moisten, add salt and pepper to taste and some chopped fresh dill or parsley. Pack this mixture into the empty peppers, cover with the cut-off tops and arrange in a shallow baking dish. Add some more stock, enough to come halfway up the peppers, and bake at 190°C/375F/Gas 5 until the peppers are tender, between 30 and 45 minutes.

To serve, take the peppers from the pan, arrange on a flat dish and pour over them either cold sour cream, tomato sauce (see pages 196–7), or a mixture of both.

The meat used in this recipe is better if raw, but cooked meat may also be used.

Salted Herrings

Syyel'd' Solyenaya

All types of salted fish are used extensively in Russia. Both filleted and unfilleted salted herrings are available. If the herrings are not filleted, they require to be soaked in milk or water for several hours, the tail and head cut off and the flesh carefully taken from the bones. Arrange this on a plate as far as possible in the original shape, with the head and tail back where they belong. Pour over the herring a mixture of oil and vinegar, or just vinegar, and garnish with sliced onion, hard-boiled eggs and black olives.

Salted herrings are eaten as an accompaniment to vodka and are also served with boiled potatoes, more especially with potatoes baked in their skins, and with salads.

RUSSIAN cooking

Salted Herring Salad (Minced)

Syel'd' Rublyenaya

1 salted herring
1 slice bread, soaked in milk
25g (1oz) unsalted butter
1 small finely chopped onion

1 large sour apple
1 cooked potato
Pepper to taste

Garnish

Chopped fresh parsley
A few slices apple

Black olives
Sliced hard-boiled egg

Soak the herring for several hours in milk, tea or water. Wash thoroughly. Cut off the head and tail. Put aside. Take the flesh from the bones and finely chop it. Grate the apple into cold water. Drain before using. Chop the potato. Squeeze the bread dry. Mix the herring, butter, onion, apple, bread and potato together and rub through a mincer. Mould this into the shape of the fish, using the head and tail to complete the illusion.

Garnish with sliced apples, parsley, black olives and egg.

Salted Herring with Garnish

Syel'd' S Garnirom

Salted herrings, filleted
1 thinly sliced onion
2 hard-boiled eggs
Pickled cucumbers

Pickled mushrooms
Strips of cooked beetroot
Capers
Cooked sliced potatoes

Soak the herrings for several hours in water or, better still, milk. Wash well, then place the fillets together so as to produce the original shape of the fish. Arrange on a small, oval service dish. Garnish with sliced onion, sliced hard-boiled eggs and pickled (or fresh) cucumbers, pickled mushrooms, strips of beetroot, capers or potatoes.

Salted herrings may also be soaked in a weak solution of tea. Milk gives the herrings a slightly milder flavour.

Chicken Livers in Sour Cream Sauce

Kurinaya Pyechyenka V Smyetannom Sousye

This and the following recipe are both popular restaurant dishes.

100g (4oz) chicken livers	Salt and pepper
25g (1oz) butter	Grated Cheddar cheese
75g (3oz) sour cream	

Clean the livers and pour boiling water over them. Melt the butter and lightly fry the livers. Add the sour cream, salt and pepper and simmer for 5 minutes. Pour the livers and the sauce into a small dish. Sprinkle over the top a small quantity of grated cheese, add any of the butter which may remain in the pan after frying the livers, and bake for a few minutes at 190°C/375°F/Gas 5.
   Serves 1 to 2 people.

Chicken Livers in Madeira

Kurinaya Pyechyenka V Sousye S Madyeroy

100g (4oz) chicken livers	150ml (1/4 pint) Madeira sauce
25g (1oz) sliced button	25g (1oz) butter
mushrooms	Chopped fresh parsley

Clean the livers by pouring boiling water over them. Melt the butter, lightly fry the livers, add the mushrooms and continue simmering in the butter for just 5 minutes. Add the sauce, bring the mixture to the boil, turn into a hot dish and sprinkle with the parsley.

Madeira Sauce

40g (1 1/2oz) butter	Salt and pepper
25g (1oz) plain flour	Madeira
Boiling vegetable stock	

Melt the butter and add the flour. Cook, stirring all the time, until the flour is a golden brown. Add enough stock to make a thick sauce and enough Madeira to thin it. Add salt and pepper to taste.

It is probably better to make the sauce before starting on the livers. Any extra sauce can be used in another dish.

Enough for 1 to 2 people.

Chicken Liver Pâté

Pashtyet Iz Pyechyenki

450g (1lb) chicken livers
100g (4oz) butter
1 carrot
chopped fresh parsley

1 small onion
1 bay leaf
peppercorns

Clean the vegetables and slice thinly. Scald the livers. Melt half the butter, lightly fry the livers until half done, this is important otherwise the pâté will be too dry. Take from the pan, add the vegetables and the parsley and cook these without any water, simply in butter, until very soft. Mix the livers, cooked vegetables, bay leaf and peppercorns and mince well. Put into a small saucepan, add remainder of the butter and cook very gently for a few minutes. Press the pâté into an earthenware jar, cool, then chill and serve cold.

The pâté is usually turned out of the mould to serve, and garnished with slices of hard-boiled eggs.

The addition of a small quantity of brandy helps the flavour, or a little brandy poured into the earthenware bowl and set alight the pâté being put in while it is still alight.

Pâté Lithuanian Style

Yakninye

450g (1lb) liver
50g (2oz) butter
50g (2oz) finely chopped onion
2–3 tablespoons red wine

Pepper and salt
Extra butter to lightly fry
the onion

Clean and scald the liver and cut into pieces. Melt the butter for frying and lightly fry the onion until soft, but not brown. Add the liver and simmer. Do not overcook or the pâté will be dry. Put the liver and onion through a mincer (or liquidizer), add wine, butter, salt and pepper and beat to a fluffy mass. Put into the top of a double saucepan, and gently cook until the liver is quite cooked. Pack into small pots and chill. Serve with hot, thin toast or crisp bread, but preferably after it has been chilled for 24 hours.

Instead of red wine, sherry or brandy can be used, also a little garlic and some mixed spices.

Minced Meat with Herrings and Potatoes

Forshmak

450g (1lb) chopped, cooked
  beef or lamb
1 salted herring, soaked
  overnight
1 chopped onion
2–3 cooked and crushed
450g (1lb) potatoes

150ml (1/4 pint) sour cream or milk
2 egg yolks
2 egg whites, stiffly beaten
25g (1oz) grated Cheddar cheese
Salt and pepper
Butter
Breadcrumbs

Sauce

Tomato sauce (see pages 196–7)

Skin, fillet and chop the herring. Put through a mincer with the meat. Heat 50g (2oz) of butter and lightly fry the onion until soft but not brown. Mix this with the potatoes, meat and herring. Add the sour cream and put again through a mincer. Add the egg yolks, salt and pepper to taste, and finally fold in the egg whites. Pour this mixture into a greased baking dish, spread it out evenly, sprinkle with cheese and breadcrumbs, dot with butter and bake at 190°C/375°F/Gas 5 for 30 to 40 minutes. When the mixture begins to shrink away from the sides, pour over it a little of the sauce. Serve

RUSSIAN cooking

the remainder of the sauce in a separate bowl.
Finely chopped, rather fat bacon may also be added.

Stuffed Tomatoes
with Vegetables

Farshirovannyye Pomidory I

6 large, firm, ripe tomatoes
2–3 cooked carrots
6–8 tablespoons mixed
  cooked vegetables, (celery,
  green beans, onions)

300ml (1/2 pint) thick white sauce
  (see page 195)
1–2 beaten eggs
Plain flour
Breadcrumbs

Cut off the tops of the tomatoes, take out the centres but keep for later use.
Mix the cooked vegetables with the sauce and pack this mixture into the
tomatoes. Replace the top, fix this with a toothpick, roll the stuffed tomatoes
in beaten egg, flour and breadcrumbs and arrange in a shallow baking dish.
Rub the tomato flesh through a sieve, add to this a little water, and pour into
the bottom of the pan, just enough to prevent burning. Bake for 1 hour at
190°C/375°F/Gas 5.
Serve hot, with a sauce. Tomatoes stuffed in this fashion are considered
as a Lenten dish.

Stuffed Tomatoes with Meat

Farshirovannyye Pomidory II

6 large, firm tomatoes

Stuffing

Cold cooked veal, or chicken
Finely chopped hard-boiled eggs
Chopped fresh parsley and dill

Salt and pepper
Sauce Provençale
150ml (1/4 pint) sour cream

Cut off the tops of the tomatoes, taking care not to damage the skins.
Mix the stuffing ingredients with half the quantity of sauce and the sour

cream. Pack this mixture into the empty tomato cases. Arrange in a shallow baking dish. Pour remainder of sauce over the tomatoes. Put into a refrigerator and serve cold.

This may also be served as a main dish.

Sauce Provençale

The recipe for this was not given with the stuffed tomatoes recipe, so I have taken mine from Escoffier. Half the quantity would be sufficient, and one could use the insides of the stuffed tomatoes.

'Peel, remove the seeds and coarsely chop 12 medium tomatoes. Heat in a saucepan 125ml (4fl oz) of olive oil until it begins to smoke a little. Add the tomatoes, seasoned with pepper and salt, add a crushed garlic clove, a pinch of powdered sugar, 1 teaspoon of chopped fresh parsley, and allow to cook gently for 30 minutes. In reality, true ProvenÁale sauce is nothing but a fine fondue of tomatoes with garlic.'

Tongue in Aspic

Zalivnoy Yasyk

1 tongue	Fresh dill and parsley
1 each carrot, turnip, onion and parsnip	Salt and peppercorns
	25g (1oz) gelatine

Wash the tongue thoroughly, put into a pan with tepid water, bring slowly to the boil, skim, add the vegetables, salt, peppercorns and herbs. Cook over a moderate heat for about 2 hours (30 minutes per 450g (1lb) and 30 minutes over is the usual timing). When the tongue is tender, take from the pan, remove the skin while it is still hot, and shape it. Leave until cold.

Dissolve the gelatine (while the tongue is cooking) in a small quantity of water, add about 300ml (1/2 pint) of the strained stock. Leave this to set but when it is half-set pour it over the tongue.

When the aspic has completely set, serve the tongue garnished with salad, vegetables such as sliced tomatoes, cucumbers or lettuce, and with any of the following sauces: sour cream, horseradish and sour cream (this is especially popular), a vinegar sauce or any piquant sauce of your choice and finally hard-boiled, sliced egg.

See section on sauces, page 195.

RUSSIAN cooking

Egg Dishes
Yaichnyye Blyuda

Eggs with Apples

Yaichnitsa S Yablokami

4 eggs
1 large apple
Butter for frying

Plain flour
Salt

Wash, peel and core the apple and cut into 4 rings. Roll in flour and fry in butter, on both sides. Drop an egg on top of each apple ring and sprinkle with salt. Either continue frying until the eggs are set, or put the pan into a hot oven, or under a grill for a few minutes to complete the cooking of the egg.

Instead of dropping the eggs whole over the apples, they can be beaten first and then poured over the apples, as for making an omelette. Partially fry and finish off under a grill, or in an oven.

This is intended as a savoury dish, but the addition of sugar turns it into an unusual sweet. I have not found it necessary to put the frying pan either under a grill or in an oven to complete cooking.

Eggs with Ham

Yaitsa S Vetchinoy

2–4 eggs
2 slices ham
25g (1oz) butter
6 thinly sliced button mushrooms

300ml (1/2 pint) sour cream
Chopped fresh parsley
Salt and pepper

Melt the butter and lightly fry the ham on both sides. Add the mushrooms, fry these for a moment or so, cover with cream, add salt and pepper and bring slowly to the boil. Drop the eggs in, one at a time, sprinkle with parsley and continue cooking until the eggs are set. Serve hot.

If using small individual frying pans these can be put into the oven for a minute or so to set the eggs, or under a hot grill. Russian recipes favour this method.

Eggs with Tongue

Yaitsa S Yazykom

As above, but instead of ham use tongue, and tomato sauce instead of sour cream, but Russian style tomato sauce (see pages 196–7).

Eggs with Honey

Yaichnitsa S Myedom

2 egg yolks   1 tablespoon warmed honey
2 egg whites

Grease 2 ramekin dishes and drop 1 yolk into each (do not break the yolks). Mix the egg whites with the honey (without prior beating), pour this mixture on top of the yolks, then put into a hot oven (230°C/450°F/Gas 8) for a few minutes until the eggs are set.

Both savoury and sweet.

Eggs with Walnuts

Yaichnitsa S Oryekami

This is a walnut-flavoured omelette.

50g (2oz) chopped walnuts   Butter
4 lightly beaten eggs   Lemon juice
2 tablespoons single cream

Whisk the eggs with the cream. Melt a little butter in a pan, fry the walnuts

19

for 2 to 3 minutes, add the eggs and fry as for an omelette.

Or omit the cream and simply mix the eggs with the walnuts and fry in butter.

Sprinkle generously with lemon juice.

A similar recipe adds: 2 tablespoons of breadcrumbs and 1 tablespoon of honey. Mix the walnuts with the breadcrumbs and fry in butter for 2 to 3 minutes. Add the honey and when this is hot take the pan from the stove and pour in the eggs, mixed with the cream. Return to the heat and fry as for an ordinary omelette.

Eggs in Green Sauce

Yaichnitsa Pod Zyelyenym Sousom

4 poached eggs
25g (1oz) butter
1 level tablespoon plain flour
450ml (3/4 pint) single cream

Salt and pepper
Handful mixed chopped chives
  fresh parsley and dill

The eggs may be poached in any manner preferred. Keep them hot. Melt the butter, stir in the flour, salt and pepper to taste, chives, parsley and dill. Gradually stir in the cream, to make a thick sauce. Drop the eggs into the sauce and serve immediately.

Or, pour the sauce into a casserole, add the poached eggs and reheat for a few minutes in a hot oven (230°C/450°F/Gas 8).

Baked Eggs I

Yaitsa V Chashkye I

Eggs lightly beaten
Chopped, lean ham
Grated cheddar cheese
Salt and pepper

Chopped chives (optional)
Tomato sauce (see pages 196–7)
Butter

Rub generously with butter as many small ramekin dishes as required. Sprinkle the bottom of each with grated cheese and chopped ham; add 1 egg to each dish, a little more ham and cheese, salt and pepper and a sprinkling of chopped chives. Bake until the egg sets at 190°C/375°F/Gas 5.

Serve with a tomato sauce (see pages 196–7).

Baked Eggs II

Yaitsa V Chashkye II

Eggs, lightly beaten with a little single cream
Salt and pepper
Finely chopped chives
Butter

Generously grease some ramekin dishes with the butter. Add beaten eggs, flavoured with salt, pepper and chives and bake at 190°C/375°F/Gas 5.

Omelette with Sour Cream

Omlyet So Smyetanoy

3 eggs
50ml (2fl oz) sour cream

Salt and pepper
Butter

Lightly beat the eggs with the cream, add salt and pepper and fry in hot butter in the usual manner.

Serve sprinkled with chopped chives.

A very light omelette.

RUSSIAN cooking

Meringue 'Omelette' and Sour Cream

Omlyet Iz Byelkov So Smyetanoy

4 egg whites   Butter for frying
30ml (1fl oz) sour cream   Salt and pepper

Beat the egg whites until very stiff, add the sour cream, salt and pepper and fry in hot butter until the underneath side has lightly browned. Turn and fry the top side.

Serve with fried tomatoes and bacon.

Stuffed Eggs

Farshirovannyye Yaitsa

Cook in boiling water as many eggs as required for 10 minutes. Take from the pan and cool under cold running water. Shell and slice lengthways into halves. Carefully remove the yolks. Chop the yolks and flavour with salt and pepper, chopped fresh dill or parsley and enough raw egg or fresh single cream to cream the mixture. Return this to the empty egg white cases. Sprinkle each egg with a little fine breadcrumbs, top with a sliver of butter, and bake at 190°C/325°F/Gas 5 for about 5 minutes. This allows the top to form a thin crust and the eggs to reheat. Serve hot.

Instead of dill or parsley, finely chopped chives may be used.

Eggs in 'Baskets' with Ham and Onions

Yaitsa V Korzinochkakh S Vyetchinoy I Lukom

6 poached eggs	6 pastry shells, or vol-au-vent
1 small, chopped onion	cases
2–3 tablespoons chopped ham	Tomato sauce (see pages 196–7)
Chopped mushroom to taste	Chopped fresh parsley or dill
Butter	Salt and pepper

Melt a little butter, lightly fry the onion and, when soft, add the ham and sauce, with salt and pepper to taste. Pour this mixture into the pastry cases, add the poached eggs, chopped mushrooms and parsley. Put in the oven long enough to reheat. Serve hot.

This same filling can be used with large, firm tomatoes.

RUSSIAN cooking

Mushrooms
Griby

For many centuries mushrooms have formed a part of the staple diet of the Russians. Consequently it is natural that the Russians eat many varieties of fungus which culinarily less adventurous people avoid mainly because they fear poisoning. Mushrooms which in Europe are sold for the millionaire's table are sold for a song in Russia. Dried mushrooms are sold in their season on the streets of Moscow, threaded on strings.

To the Russians the finest enjoyment to be had from mushrooms (apart, obviously, from their eating) is in the gathering of them at dawn, when the morning mist still lies on the ground; or on lovely autumn days after the first gentle rains. The annual search under the trees for mushrooms of every description in the great pine and birch forests is an occasion to which everyone looks forward. Early Russian novelists have written in glowing terms of the gaily clad peasants going out into the countryside, their mushroom baskets hanging on their arms, heads warmly tied in coloured handkerchiefs, singing mournful Russian songs which echoed through the woods, as they walked or gathered mushrooms. In such an atmosphere heavy with song and emotion were the mushrooms gathered.

Well, probably these were exaggerated descriptions, but certainly today, with fewer songs and less emotion, the mushrooms are still gathered and their gathering is still an event. No one would hesitate to cancel an important engagement if it should fall on the day of the mushroom gathering.

Some of the mushrooms gathered in the early dewy morning are eaten the same day. But most are dried, salted or pickled, ready for the sterner winter months to follow.

The Russians and the Poles both have a large variety of wild mushrooms. When dried mushrooms are recommended for Russian recipes I would suggest using the Polish dried variety, if available, rather than the Italian, which, although excellent, are cultivated mushrooms, and therefore of a quite different flavour. I also used dried mushrooms from Kashmir.

Marinated Mushrooms

Marinovannyye Griby

For this recipe the best type of mushrooms are the small, white ones.

900g (2lb) small mushrooms	2 bay leaves
600ml (1 pint) vinegar and	1 tablespoon coarse salt
water mixed	1 teaspoon peppercorns

Wash the mushrooms, remove the stalks and cook gently in hot, salted water until tender. Drain and leave until quite cold.

Bring the vinegar and water mixture with the bay leaves and peppercorns to the boil, simmer for 10 minutes and leave until cold. Strain.

Pack the mushrooms into jars, add the vinegar and water mixture and cover tightly. Leave for several days before using.

Or pack the mushrooms while still hot into scalded jars, cover with the marinade, seal tightly and leave for 2 weeks in a cool place before using.

The quantity of vinegar depends on individual taste. Use all vinegar if preferred. Although small mushrooms are the best for such pickling, field mushrooms which are undamaged and not too large may also be used. A little minced onion is often added to the vinegar while it is cooking.

In the days before the Russian Revolution mushrooms were picked by the barrel.

RUSSIAN cooking

Salted Mushrooms

Solyenyye Griby

Mushrooms
Salt

Cold water

1. Soak the mushrooms in cold water for 4 days. Put into a cask in layers, each layer liberally sprinkled with salt. Add boiled but cold water. Cover tightly and put into a cold place. Ready for use in 6 weeks time.

2. Wash and dry the mushrooms, cut into pieces according to the size of the mushrooms, pack the pieces carefully into a cask (remembering they will shrink), sprinkle each layer with salt, add chopped onion and a few peppercorns. Cover the cask tightly and keep in a cool place.

Failing a wooden cask, use an earthenware jar.

Mushroom 'Caviar'

Gribnaya Ikra

50g (2oz) dried mushrooms
225g (8oz) salted mushrooms
1 small onion, minced
Crushed garlic to taste
Olive oil

Lemon juice
Pepper
Minced spring onions to taste
Finely chopped fresh parsley

The dried mushrooms must be soaked overnight. Chop both salted and dried mushrooms into fairly small pieces.

Heat a little oil, simmer the onion and, when this begins to soften, add the mushrooms. Simmer until tender, about 10 minutes; take from the pan, cool and mash to a pulp. Add the garlic, and enough oil and lemon juice (as when making a dressing), a little of each until the mixture is a thick spread. Add pepper, sprinkle generously with parsley and spring onions. Serve with soft, coarse brown bread.

The 'caviar' is usually served in a small dish.

Mushroom caviar is also prepared from only salted or only dried mushrooms.

Mushrooms with Kidneys

Pochki S Gribami

450g (1lb) mushrooms
1 tablespoon minced onion
50–75g (2–3oz) butter
300ml (1/2 pint) sour cream

Salt and pepper to taste
225g (8oz) kidney soaked
  in milk for 1 hour

Melt the butter, lightly fry the onion, add the mushrooms and simmer gently. Drain the kidneys, slice and add to the pan. Stir in the sour cream, add salt and pepper to taste and cook these ingredients gently until the kidney is tender. If a thicker sauce is required, sprinkle with a little plain flour 5 minutes before adding the sour cream.

Mushrooms in Sour Cream I

Griby V Smyetannom Sousye I

Wash as many small, white mushrooms as required and cook gently in a covered saucepan in a little water for 5 minutes. Pour off the liquid, add enough butter in which to simmer the mushrooms, a little finely chopped onion, some finely chopped bacon, salt and pepper and cook gently until the mushrooms are tender. At the very last moment, sprinkle in a little plain flour, stir this well into the ingredients and add enough sour cream to make a sauce. Simmer until the sauce is hot.

RUSSIAN cooking

Mushrooms in Sour Cream II

Griby V Smyetannom Sousye II

100g (4oz) dried mushrooms
25g (1oz) plain flour
300ml (½ pint) sour cream

Salt and pepper
1 teaspoon onion juice, or
  finely chopped onion

Wash the mushrooms in hot water, then soak overnight in cold water. Next morning drain and cook in a little fresh water until tender. Drain and coarsely chop.

   Mix 4 tablespoons of the sour cream with the flour, add salt and pepper and mix to a smooth paste. Add the remainder of the cream and cook over boiling water, stirring all the time, until the sauce is thick. Add the mushrooms and the onion juice. Continue to cook (still over hot water) for several minutes, taking care the sauce does not curdle.

Mushrooms with Potatoes

Griby Tushyennyye S Kartofyelyem

450g (1lb) firm mushrooms
225g (8oz) potatoes, cooked
  in their skins
90ml (3fl oz) tomato sauce
  (see pages 196–7) or sour cream

100g (4oz) butter
1 small onion, chopped
Pinch nutmeg
Chopped fresh dill to taste

Wash and slice the mushrooms. Peel and dice the potatoes.

   Melt half the butter, fry the mushrooms for a few minutes, add sauce and simmer for 15 minutes, or until the mushrooms are tender. In another pan heat the remaining butter and lightly fry the onion and potatoes. Add these to the mushrooms. Add salt and peppercorns, chopped dill and nutmeg and simmer a few minutes before serving.

Stuffed Mushrooms

Farshirovannyye Griby

225g (8oz) large, firm
  mushrooms
3–4 firm tomatoes
Olive oil for frying
A little chopped onion.

Crushed garlic to taste
Breadcrumbs
Chopped fresh dill and/or parsley
Salt and pepper

Remove the stalks from the mushrooms and carefully scoop out part of the flesh from the caps. Heat a little oil and fry the caps. Take from the pan and keep hot. Finely chop the removed mushroom flesh and the stalks. Fry this together with the onion until soft. Add the garlic and herbs, salt and pepper and enough soft breadcrumbs to bind the mixture. Fill the mushroom caps with this.

Slice the tomatoes, as many thick slices as mushroom caps. Either fry these in oil, or bake in a hot oven (230°C/450°F/Gas 8). Serve 1 stuffed mushroom on each slice of tomato.

RUSSIAN cooking

Soups
Supy

There are Russian soups for all occasions. For cold days they are hot and rich, usually with a basis of meat and vegetables, or fish with sauerkraut or cabbage. The famous Russian sour cucumber dish of solyanka would be considered by most of us as a stew or a chowder.

An important ingredient in Russian soups, especially in borshch (which is usually made at least 24 hours before it is required, and is reheated) is kvas, a fermented liquor (see page 000). This is not only the basis for a good borshch but also for some of the hot weather soups, like okroshka.

Of all the Russian soups borshch is the most internationally famed, and it varies as much as a recipe possibly can vary. There are thick and thin borshchs as well as hot and cold. One borshch is so clear and light in colour it is almost a consommé of chicken broth with beetroot colouring. All borshchs must be served with a sour cream dressing.

Fish soups of all kinds are exceedingly popular. A favourite is sterlet soup.

In Russia, soups usually have a thin film of fat floating over the top. This comes from the heavy use of fat when frying the vegetables. There is no need to emulate this film.

Borsh, Moscow-style

Borsh Moskovskii I

Clear beef stock (enough for
  8 people)
225g (8oz) ham-bone
450g (1lb) raw beetroots
225g (8oz) potatoes
450g (1lb) cabbage
2 carrots
1/2 parsnip (optional)

2 onions
1 tablespoon tomato purée
25g (1oz) butter
Chopped fresh parsley to taste
Salt, pepper and sugar
1 tablespoon vinegar
Sour cream

Strain the stock into a pan, add the ham-bone and bring to the boil over a moderate heat. While it is cooking wash and grate the beetroots. Add these to the stock. Add the vinegar, bring the stock again to the boil, then put on the side of the stove for 20 minutes.

Prepare the remaining vegetables. Wash and shred the cabbage, peel and chop the potatoes, parsnip and onions. Peel and shred the carrots.

Melt the butter and lightly fry the vegetables. Add the tomato purée, stir well, add salt, pepper and sugar. Transfer this mixture to the soup. Bring once more to the boil, then cook slowly for 30 to 40 minutes.

Take out the ham-bone. If there is any edible meat on it, cut this into small pieces and return to the soup. Add the parsley. Tiny Frankfurter sausages may also be added to this kind of borshch.

Before serving, pour into each plate of soup, 1 tablespoon of sour cream.

Simple Borsh

Borshch II

900g (2lb) stewing steak
450g (1lb) beetroots
Bunch fresh dill
600ml (1 pint) kvas, dry cider
  or beer (see page 229)

Salt
Sour cream
Chopped fresh dill
  to taste

Wash and cut the meat into large chunks. Put into a large pot with the beetroots, dill and 2.3 litres (4 pints) of salted water and cook over a moderate heat until the beetroots are tender. Take these out (let the soup continue cooking) and, as soon as you can handle, peel and grate them. Then return to the pot with the kvas, beer or cider. Continue cooking until you have cooked the meat for 3 hours. Strain and serve the soup, offering sour cream separately.

If not using either kvas, beer or cider, add instead 2 tablespoons of good quality vinegar.

Enough for 6 to 8 people.

RUSSIAN cooking

Borsh, Ukrainian-style

Borshch Ukrainskii III

1.7 litres (3 pints) chicken stock
225g (8oz) beetroot, cooked and cut
  as thinly as matchsticks
2–3 potatoes, cut into cubes
1 small cabbage, finely shredded
225g (8oz) whole fresh tomatoes
Sour cream

2 onions, minced
1 bay leaf
2 rashers very fat bacon,
  chopped and without rind
2 tablespoons vinegar
Salt and pepper

Bring the stock and vinegar to the boil, add the beetroots and boil until these are almost white; then add the potatoes. After 10 minutes add the cabbage and tomatoes. When the tomatoes are soft, take them from the pan and rub through a sieve back into the soup. Add bay leaf and salt and pepper to taste. Mince the onions with the fat bacon and add to the soup; continue to cook for about 20 minutes. Serve with sour cream.

The Ukrainians are credited with having invented borsh.

Cold Borsh

Kholodnyi Borshch IV

3 or 4 beetroots
450g (1lb) cooked and diced potatoes
1 sliced or diced small cucumber
50g (2oz) chopped spring onions
2 tablespoons wine vinegar

1 tablespoon sugar
1–2 chopped, hard-boiled
  egg yolks
Salt and pepper
Sour cream

Peel the beetroots, cut into small pieces and put into a pot with 1.2 litres (2 pints) of water and the vinegar and bring to the boil. Cook until the beets are tender and leave until cold. Add the potatoes, cucumber, hard-boiled egg yolks and the spring onions, salt, pepper and sugar and garnish when in the plates with sour cream.

Another way is to grate the beetroot and cook it with the beetroot leaves, but straining the liquid before leaving it to cool.

The remaining vegetables are interchangeable. Grated carrots are sometimes used in this type of soup, also tomatoes, celery or parsnip, it is a matter of using what is available.

Cold Borsh, Siberian-style

Kholodnyi Borshch V

1.2 litres (2 pints) buttermilk
4 cooked egg yolks
Thinly sliced or diced cucumber
2 chopped or shredded cooked
  beetroots

Salt and pepper
Fresh dill, finely chopped
Lemon juice to taste

Mash the egg yolks and beat into the buttermilk. Cook the mixture over hot water until it thickens, stirring all the time. Cool, add salt, pepper and lemon juice. Leave in the refrigerator, or in a really cold place until chilled. Just before serving add the remaining ingredients.

Fresh or pickled cucumber may be used in this recipe.

Fish Borsh

Rybnyi Borshch

Make a well-flavoured fish stock, follow any recipe, although to be correct the stock should be prepared from a mixture of fish, in which sea perch or bass figure as the main flavour. Strain the stock.

Fish stock
Small pieces fried fish

Sour cream
Chopped fresh dill, or parsley (or both)

The fish should be cut into pieces small enough to be eaten easily (the size of the average crouton served in soup) and fried in butter until a golden brown. These pieces are dropped into the simmering stock, and the soup is served as soon as all the pieces of fish are in the soup and reheated.

Serve hot, sprinkled with dill or parsley, and with a tablespoon of sour cream in each plate.

RUSSIAN cooking

This is really one of the simplest soups to make, especially as quantities are all 'as required'.

Instead of fried pieces of fish, fried shrimps or prawns can be used.

Cold Soup

Okroshka I

Okroshka is usually thought of as a cucumber soup. It is popular not only with the Russians but also with those foreigners who live in Russia, and is frequently served in Moscow restaurants where foreigners eat.

225g (8oz) finely chopped,
  cooked beef or lamb
225g (8oz) finely chopped,
  cooked ham
225g (8oz) finely chopped veal
2–3 small cucumbers
4 chopped spring onions

4 tablespoons sour cream
1–2 chopped, hard-boiled eggs
1 teaspoon English mustard powder
Finely chopped fresh dill and parsley
Kvas, dry cider, beer or white wine
  white wine (see page 229)
Salt

Note

The cucumbers should be chopped or sliced, marinated in salt for about 2 hours and wiped dry. The meat must be chopped, not minced.

Put all the ingredients (except the eggs) in the order given into a soup tureen, or a large bowl and chill for 4 hours. Add the hard-boiled eggs just before serving.

Instead of beef, chopped or whole shrimps can be used.

Cold Soup with White Wine

Okroshka II

Put into a soup tureen 1 tablespoon of finely chopped fresh dill, 1 tablespoon of finely chopped chives and half that quantity of chopped fresh parsley. Add salt, pepper and sugar to taste but not more than a teaspoon of any, particularly of the pepper. Mix these ingredients, then add

4 tablespoons of sour cream, 1 teaspoon of French mustard, some small, whole shrimps (about 600ml (1 pint) of these), 2 to 3 peeled, diced or sliced cucumbers (marinated in salt), 600ml (1 pint) of strained, cold chicken consommé, 600ml (1 pint) of dry white wine and 300ml (1/2 pint) of iced water. Chill until absolutely ice-cold. Just before serving, sprinkle in 2 finely chopped hard-boiled egg yolks.

The quantity of shrimps may be reduced if sufficiently diced cold meats are added to make up the quantity.

Cold Vegetable Soup

Okroshka III

1.7 litres (3 pints) kvas
  light beer or wine (see page 229)
2 fresh cucumbers (peeled,
  sliced and marinated in salt)
4–5 radishes
1–2 boiled, cold potatoes
2–3 spring onions
2 hard-boiled eggs

1/2 teaspoon salt (or as taste
  dictates)
1/2 teaspoon English mustard
  powder
4 tablespoons sour cream
1/2 teaspoon sugar
Chopped fresh dill and parsley

Dice the potatoes; trim and slice the radishes, finely chop the spring onions, using as much of the green as possible. Shell the eggs, cut them into halves and scoop out the yolks; finely chop the whites. Combine the minced spring onions with the potatoes, cucumbers, chopped egg whites and salt. Mash the egg yolks and mix these with the mustard; work this mixture into the sour cream and mix with the vegetables, etc. Stir into this the kvas, beer or wine, sprinkle with chopped dill and parsley, or either of each, and serve exceedingly cold, an ice cube floating in each plate.

Other vegetables than those mentioned may be used but it is essential to use cucumber.

The wine or the beer can be diluted with water. While this may not be palatable to drink, it works perfectly well in the soup ... and, of course, dry cider may be used instead.

If using the English size cucumber, half of one of average size will be sufficient.

RUSSIAN cooking

Fish Soup

Ukha

700g (1½lb) fish
2 bay leaves
1 large, chopped onion
2 chopped carrots
About 2–3 litres (4 pints) water

Salt and peppercorns to taste
Butter for frying
Chopped fresh dill
Lemon juice

Bone the fish and put most of the flesh aside. Put the bones, head and a little of the flesh into a large saucepan. Add the water, onion, carrots, bay leaves, salt and peppercorns and bring to the boil. Reduce the heat and simmer gently for 1 hour.

While the stock is cooking, cut the remaining fish into small pieces and lightly fry this in butter. Strain the soup, return it to the pan, add the fried fish and bring the soup once more to the boil. Sprinkle with lemon juice and chopped dill. Serve hot.

Such soups are often thickened with a flour and stock paste. After straining the stock, but before adding the fish pieces, add a paste made from 1 level tablespoon of plain flour mixed with some of the strained stock. Stir this into the soup, then continue to cook until the soup has thickened and the flour is properly cooked (at least another 5 minutes) before adding the fish.

The original recipe called for pike, salmon, perch or sturgeon. Other fish may be substituted. Olive oil may be used instead of butter for frying.

Crayfish Soup

Rakovyi Sup

2 x 200g (7oz) tins crayfish,
  or crabmeat
25g (1oz) butter
25g (1oz) plain flour
1.2 litres (2 pints) fish stock
2 egg yolks

2 tablespoons fresh cream
Salt and pepper
300ml (½ pint) milk
2 bay leaves
Chopped fresh dill and parsley
Few caraway seeds (optional)

Take out some of the larger pieces of the crayfish (or crabmeat) and put these aside for garnishing. Chop the remainder. Put the stock, the liquid from the tins, the bay leaves, dill and parsley, salt, pepper and caraway seeds into a pan and cook over a moderate heat for about 20 minutes.

In another pan, melt the butter, stir in the flour and gradually add the milk. Bring this to the boil, stirring all the while. Strain the stock and pour this slowly into the white sauce. Add the chopped fish and cook gently for 15–20 minutes. While this is simmering, beat the egg yolks with the cream, take the pan from the heat and stir this mixture into the soup. Add the garnishing pieces, return to the heat, stir and cook slowly until the soup almost comes to the boil. Serve hot.

This is a modern version of a very famous old Russian recipe, which begins with instructions for 'first catch your crayfish'.

'Green' Fish Soup (Baltic-Russian)

Borvin'ya

100g (4oz) each spinach, sorrel
  and lettuce leaves
50g (2oz) pickled cucumbers,
  thinly sliced
Salt and pepper
1 tablespoon sugar
4 tablespoons finely chopped
  fresh dill, parsley and chives (mixed)

1 teaspoon grated horseradish
1.2 litres (2 pints) kvas
  (see page 229), or dry white
  wine, cider or beer
Cold, cooked fish, preferably hake,
  pike, roach or cod as required
Lemon rind

Wash the spinach, sorrel and lettuce leaves very carefully and chop finely. Cook in a little boiling water until tender, then rub through a sieve into a soup tureen, or large bowl. Add the lemon rind, salt, pepper, sugar, horseradish, herbs and finally the kvas, wine, cider or beer. Add to it several cubes of ice and leave in a refrigerator until required. Just before serving, add the cucumber and fish, which should be cut into small pieces.

In the old days the fish and the cucumber was served separately.

The amount of kvas, wine, cider or beer can be reduced by mixing it with water, iced chicken consommé or vegetable stock, adding only enough fermented liquid to flavour.

Serve cold. Chopped shellfish may be added.

RUSSIAN cooking

Fish Chowder

Rybnaya Solyanka

700g (1½lb) any type coarse fish
4–5 pickled cucumbers
1–2 onions
2–3 tomatoes
1 tablespoon capers
1 tablespoon black olives

50g (2oz) butter
1 bay leaf and 1 clove
½ sliced lemon
Fresh dill and parsley, chopped
Salt and peppercorns

A *solyanka* is usually made with a 'red' fish such as sturgeon or some member of the sturgeon family. The fish must be skinned and filleted.

Put the bones, skin and head with 2.3 litres (4 pints) of water into a pan to make a stock, add a little onion, a clove and bayleaf, salt and peppercorns. Strain.

Peel and chop the onions. Cut the fish into pieces. Slice the cucumbers, peel and slice the tomatoes. Stone and chop the olives.

In a saucepan, melt the butter and lightly fry the onion; when this begins to change colour, add the tomatoes and cook gently for about 6 minutes. Add the fish, cucumbers, peppercorns, capers, and finally the stock. Bring this to the boil, lower the heat and cook over a moderate heat for 15 minutes, or until the fish is tender. Just before serving add the olives, lemon, dill and parsley.

In all of the *solyanka* dishes salted cucumbers or sauerkraut is essential.

Georgian Beef Soup

Sup Kharcho Po-gruzinski

450–900g (1–2lb) beef,
  preferably brisket
1–2 large, sliced onions
1 tablespoon tomato purée
2–3 cloves garlic, chopped
50g (2oz) long-grain rice
2 tablespoons chopped
  fresh chives

¼ teaspoon dried mixed
  herbs
100g (4oz) prunes
Salt and pepper
Finely chopped fresh dill,
  or parsley
1 tablespoon wine vinegar

Cut the beef into fairly small pieces and put into a pan with 2.3 litres (4 pints) of water and the dried herbs. Bring to the boil, skim off surplus fat and simmer until the meat is tender. Add the sliced onions, chives, garlic, rice, tomato purée (or fresh, peeled tomatoes), salt and pepper and continue cooking until these ingredients are cooked. Just before serving, sprinkle with finely chopped dill, or parsley and stir in the vinegar.

This soup, which is in the stew class, has some resemblance to soup called *Ache*.

Armenian Soup

Vospi Apur

350g (12oz) beef or lamb
175g (6oz) green lentils
275g (10oz) potatoes
50g (2oz) butter
25g (1oz) plain flour

75g (3oz) coarsely ground walnuts
75g (3oz) dried apricots or prunes
 (previously soaked)
Salt and pepper
Fresh dill or fennel

Soak the lentils overnight or for a few hours.

Cut the meat into 6 pieces and put into a pan with plenty of water, salt and pepper to taste and bring to the boil. Drain the lentils, add to the boiling stock and cook until these are soft and the meat is tender.

Peel and cube the potatoes. Melt the butter, add the potatoes, sprinkle these with flour and cook until just brown. Add to the soup, then add the soaked fruit and walnuts; cook until potatoes and fruit are soft. Serve very hot with a piece of meat in each plate, sprinkled with finely chopped dill or fennel, fennel is more usual in this kind of soup.

Apricots and prunes can be mixed, and the prunes must, of course, be stoned.

An unusual soup, more like a stew, but very pleasant on a cold, wet day. Failing dill or fennel, parsley may be used, or any equally flavoured herb.

RUSSIAN cooking

Salted Cucumber and Kidney Soup

Rassol'nik S Pochkami

2.3 litres (4 pints) strained
  beef or lamb stock
4 kidneys
25g (1oz) dried mushrooms
  (optional)
225g (8oz) finely shredded red
  cabbage

3 peeled and quartered
  potatoes
2–3 diced pickled cucumbers
1 beaten egg yolk
150ml (1/4 pint) sour cream

If using dried mushrooms, wash them well, scald and soak in a little water for several hours, or overnight.

Trim the kidneys, slice and put into a saucepan with cold water and bring to the boil. Strain, rinse the kidneys and return to the pan, in fresh cold water. Bring again to the boil and simmer until the kidneys are tender. Strain, and slice when cool enough to handle.

Meanwhile bring the stock to the boil, chop the mushrooms and add (with their liquid) to the boiling stock. Add the red cabbage, potatoes and cucumbers. When these ingredients are tender, add the kidneys. Beat the egg yolk into the sour cream and carefully stir this into the soup. Cook for 3 minutes over a low heat before serving.

While adding the egg yolk and cream it is safer to have the pan off the heat to avoid curdling.

For those who live in the country, garden sorrel, or even lettuce, may be used instead of the red cabbage. A little vinegar is often added to make the soup even more sour.

Like so many Russian soups, this one is often served sprinkled with either chopped fresh dill or parsley and sometimes instead of mixing egg yolk with the sour cream, the yolks are chopped and sprinkled on top of the soup, and the sour cream is served separately.

Mutton Soup *(Uzbekistan)*

Shurpa-chaban

700g (1 1/2lb) lamb for
  making stock
2–3 large potatoes
2 large onions
2 large tomatoes

Olive oil for frying
Finely chopped fresh dill,
  or parsley
Salt and pepper

Clean and cut the meat into pieces and put into a saucepan with 2.3 litres (4 pints) of water, salt and pepper. Cook over a moderate heat until the liquid is reduced by a quarter. Take out the meat and, as soon as you can handle it, cut it into very small pieces.

While the meat is cooking prepare the vegetables. Peel and dice the potatoes and tomatoes and chop the onions finely.

Heat the oil and lightly fry the onions until soft but not brown; add the meat, brown this; finally add the tomatoes and continue frying for about 5 minutes. Pour this mixture into the stock, stirring all the time; then add the potatoes and continue cooking until these are soft. Sprinkle with dill or parsley before serving.

Russians often use fat from the stock, which they skim off the top. Some recipes only fry half the meat and vegetables and, of course, the calorie conscious may put them into the soup without frying at all, although this obviously changes the character of the soup.

Most of the eastern style soups are very rich and are frequently served in Russia with blobs of mutton fat floating on the top.

Cabbage Soup

Shchi

2–3 litres (4 pints) vegetable
  stock
About 450g (1lb) shredded white
  cabbage
2 finely chopped onions
2 sliced carrots

Chopped celery or celeriac to taste
Salt and pepper
150ml (1/4 pint) sour cream
1 level tablespoon plain flour
Finely chopped fresh dill or
  parsley

RUSSIAN cooking

Bring the stock to the boil in a large pan, add the carrots, onions and celery and cook for 15 minutes. Add the cabbage and cook until all these ingredients are tender; add salt and pepper if required. Take some of the stock from the pan, mix this into the flour to make a paste and stir it into the sour cream. Pour this mixture slowly into the soup, stirring all the time, until it reaches boiling point. Immediately reduce the heat and simmer for a further 3 minutes. Sprinkle with dill and parsley just before serving.

To make the soup more filling (although it is filling enough as it is) add peeled, chopped tomatoes and potatoes.

'Lazy' Cabbage Soup

Shchi Lyenivyye

1 large white cabbage
2 carrots
2 parsnips
1 leek
Handful finely chopped fresh
  parsley and fresh dill

2–3 litres (4 pints) vegetable stock
25g (1oz) butter
1 level tablespoon plain flour
Salt and pepper
Sour cream

Clean the cabbage and cut into 8 pieces. Leave soaking for about 1 hour. Peel and chop the carrots, parsnips and leek. Drop these into boiling, salted water and cook over a medium heat for about 5 minutes.

Drain the cabbage and put it into a pan with the stock. Add salt and pepper. Strain the remaining vegetables and add these to the pan. Cook until all the vegetables are tender, about 15 to 20 minutes. Strain off 300ml (1/2 pint) of the liquid.

Melt the butter, stir in the flour and, when smooth, add the strained liquid. Stir this back into the soup and bring once more to the boil. Serve, generously sprinkled with finely chopped parsley and dill and sour cream.

Sometimes potatoes and tomatoes are added to the soup.

The 'laziness' consists of cutting the cabbage into large pieces, instead of shredding it.

Sauerkraut Soup

Kislyye Shchi

450g (1lb) sauerkraut
1 finely chopped onion
1 bay leaf
50g (2oz) fat bacon or salt
    fat pork

2–3 litres (4 pints) seasoned
    beef or lamb stock
150ml (1/4 pint) sour cream

Chop the sauerkraut so that it is even more finely shredded than usual. Cook the bacon, or pork, add the onion and, when this begins to turn a pinky brown, add the sauerkraut and simmer for 15 minutes. Add the bay leaf and a little of the stock and continue to cook over a moderate heat for another 15 minutes before adding the remainder of the stock. Continue to cook for another hour and, just before serving, stir in the sour cream.

It is usual to make this soup the day before it is required. Reheating brings out the fullness of its flavour. If the flavour of sauerkraut seems a little sharp, add a teaspoon of sugar just towards the end of cooking.

Cream of Dried Mushroom Soup

Gribnoy Sup

50g (2oz) dried white mushrooms
2 finely chopped onions
6 peppercorns
1 tablespoon plain flour
1 tablespoon plain flour
1 beaten egg yolk

2 tablespoons sour cream
Salt to taste
1–2 hard-boiled egg yolks,
    finely chopped
Handful chopped fresh parsley

The evening before the soup is required wash the mushrooms in hot water and soak overnight in 600ml (1 pint) of water. Bring 1.2 litres (2 pints) of water to the boil, add the onions, some parsley, peppercorns and salt and let this cook for 30 minutes. Strain and keep the stock hot. Drain the mushrooms and keep the liquid in which they have been soaking, and chop them finely. In a large saucepan, melt the butter and lightly fry the mushrooms. Sprinkle in the flour, stirring it into the butter and mushrooms, then add 225ml (8fl oz) of the onion stock to the pan. Cook for 15 minutes over a slow heat. Add the liquid in which the mushrooms have been soaked, plus the remaining onion stock and bring it all slowly to the boil. Beat the egg yolk with the sour cream and add this carefully to the soup (with the pan off the heat) just before serving. Sprinkle some more parsley into the soup and, once the soup is in the plates, garnish it with finely chopped hard-boiled egg yolk.

Potato and Sorrel Soup
(Baltic-Russian)

Sup Kartofylel'nyi So Shchavyelyem

4 large potatoes
1.2 litres (3 pints) vegetable stock
450g (1lb) sorrel

25g (1oz) butter (not salted)
1 egg yolk
Sour cream

Peel the potatoes and cook until soft in the stock. Rub through a sieve. Clean the sorrel and cook it without liquid until soft; chop and add to the soup. Cook uncovered for about 30 minutes. Beat the egg yolk with the butter and stir this mixture carefully into the soup. Serve hot with sour cream.

Failing sorrel, and for this recipe it should be garden sorrel, use spinach to which has been added a good teaspoon of lemon juice.

Tomato Soup with Sour Cream

Sup Iz Pomidorov

900g (2lb) tomatoes, coarsely chopped
2.3 litres (4 pints) vegetable stock
300ml (1/2 pint) sour cream
25g (1oz) plain flour

1 teaspoon sugar
50g (2oz) unsalted butter
Salt and pepper
Chopped fresh dill or parsley

Melt the butter, add the tomatoes and cook over a low heat until very soft. Rub through a sieve. Return the purée to the pan. Stir in all but 250ml (8fl oz) of the stock. Cook for about 30 minutes.

Mix the flour with the remaining stock to a smooth paste and stir this into the soup. Add salt and pepper if required. Just before serving, add the sugar and the sour cream. Cook over a low heat for another 3 or 4 minutes.

Sprinkle with chopped dill or parsley.

Apple and Pear Soup
(Fresh Fruit Soup)

Sup Iz Svyezhikh Fruktov

450g (1lb) cooking apples	Sour cream
450g (1lb) cooking pears	1 teaspoon ground cinnamon
25g (1oz) cornflour	Sliced lemon (optional)
50g (2oz) sugar, or to taste	About 1.2 litres (2 pints) water

Peel and core the apples and pears and cut into smallish pieces. Put into a pan with the water and sugar and cook until soft. Rub through a sieve, return to the pan and bring to the boil. Mix the cornflour with enough cold water to make a thin paste, stir this into the soup and continue cooking gently for 5 minutes. If the soup is not sufficiently bitter, add slices of lemon or some lemon juice. Add a tablespoon of sour cream to each plate of soup.

Fruit soups of all kinds are popular, not only in Russia but in all the Baltic countries as well as Germany and central European countries. Eaten both hot and cold, they are served at the beginning of a meal.

The above is sufficient for 4 or even 6 people.

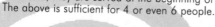

RUSSIAN cooking

Dumplings
Klyetski

Dumplings I

Klyetski I

Dumplings of all kinds are used as garnishings in many Russian soups. The following recipes are simple, not at all difficult to prepare and excellent with clear soups.

1 egg
1 good tablespoon single cream
Salt to taste

100g (4oz) unsalted butter
Plain flour
Boiling vegetable stock

Just slightly beat the egg with the cream and add salt. Cream the butter, beat this into the egg and gradually add sufficient flour to make a batter of cake consistency. Beat steadily with a wooden spoon until the batter no longer clings to the side of the bowl. Drop small portions from the tip of a teaspoon into the boiling stock. Cook for 5 minutes. Makes minute balls.

Dumplings II

Klyetski II

250g (8oz) plain flour
1 teaspoon baking powder
1/4 teaspoon salt
2 teaspoons minced onion

2 teaspoons chopped fresh
  parsley or dill
About 125ml (4fl oz) milk

Sift the dry ingredients into a bowl, add the onion and parsley and enough milk to make a soft dough of dropping consistency. Drop small portions from the tip of a teaspoon into boiling water or soup. As soon as the dumplings are all in the pan, cover and boil steadily for about 15 minutes.

The two recipes on page 46 are probably the most usual dumpling recipes for use with Russian soups. Here are some other variations:

Chicken Dumplings

Klyetski Iz Kuritsy

175g (6oz) uncooked minced
 chicken
50g (2oz) soft breadcrumbs
Milk

1 well-beaten egg
Salt and pepper to taste
50ml (2fl oz) sour cream

Soak the breadcrumbs in a little milk and squeeze free of excess liquid. Mix with the minced chicken. Add salt and pepper. Gradually add the cream. Shape the paste into balls, or minute dumplings and drop these into hot soup or water. Cook until the dumplings rise to the top of the liquid and remain there. If the dumplings mixture is too stiff, add some well-beaten egg. This will loosen the mixture and help also to bind it.

Similar dumplings may be made with other white meat.

Liver Dumplings

Klyetski Iz Pyechyenki

100g (4oz) raw liver
1 teaspoon minced onion
1 rasher streaky bacon
50g (2oz) soft breadcrumbs

1 tablespoon chopped fresh
 parsley or dill
Salt and pepper

Clean the liver and put it through a mincer with the bacon. Add the remaining ingredients. Mix well, shape into small balls and cook in boiling water or soup for about 5 minutes. This quantity makes around 30 tiny dumplings.

Although the recipe does not call for an egg, I prefer to use enough beaten egg to bind the mixture.

RUSSIAN cooking

Veal Dumplings

Klyetski Iz Tyelyatiny

175g (6oz) minced veal
1 whole egg
2 heaped tablespoons soft
  breadcrumbs

Milk
1 tablespoon minced onion

Soak the breadcrumbs in a little milk and squeeze to a smooth paste. Add remaining ingredients (the egg may be omitted), shape into tiny balls, or dumplings, and drop into boiling stock or water. Cook for 15 minutes, or until the dumplings lie lightly on the top of the soup.

    Similar dumplings may be made with pork or chicken meat.

Fish
Ryba

There are parts of Russia, principally in the northern areas, where fish forms an important part of the staple diet. Although much of the fish caught in these northern waters is eaten locally, vast quantities are smoked or salted and transported. Most Russian fish is of good quality; much of it is fresh-water fish, inclined to be looked down upon by many Britons; and almost all of it, with the possible exception of the sturgeon, is very bony.

The most important fish in Russia is, of course, the sturgeon, not only because it produces the best caviar, or rather the only genuine caviar, but also because of its own delicious flavour as a fish. It is usually served poached, with a slice of lemon, a favourite way in any case of serving fish in Russia, although it also comes to the table with a sour cream sauce or a rich wine and cherry one.

Almost as popular is salmon, of which there are several varieties in Russia. A favourite species is a rather oily variety, which is eaten as often smoked as fresh. When salmon is served fresh it is cooked in the usual, classical manner, that is, lightly poached. Very small fish are extremely popular, in particular one called *kilki*, which has been variously translated as smelt, sardine, Norwegian sardine, etc.

Herrings are not treated as the humble fish they tend to be in Britain but are given an important place on the *zakuski* table and are cooked in every possible manner.

Some Russian fish is served 'raw', that is marinated or prepared in the following manner as explained to me by a Ukrainian woman. The fish is caught in the spring 'at the parting of the rivers', by which I imagine she meant when the ice melts. Then the fishermen go out with a kind of garden fork and literally dig the fish, usually perch, out of the river banks. It is then generously rubbed with salt, to prevent its getting slimy, and is wrapped tightly in dill and fresh bay leaves, clamped between two pieces of ice and left for a long time ... until ready for eating. The flavour, she told me, is absolutely fabulous.

Another of her fishing stories concerned crayfish which abound in the Ukraine, and almost beg to be caught. As a girl my friend and her family would go to the beach and dig in the wet sands with sticks, around which

RUSSIAN cooking

were wrapped pieces of cloth. The crayfish would cling to the cloth, and, still wriggling, would be popped at once into a pan of boiling water. A crayfish picnic followed.

An unusual Russian taste is to serve fish with spring onions, as heavily flavoured with them as ours might be with lemon. The Russians have such a preference for the spring onion that they grow the bulbs in bottles and jars in their kitchens during the winter months so that when the soft green stalks sprout they can use them as a flavouring.

Cod's liver is eaten in large quantities, but it is for the foreigner an acquired taste.

Bream Stuffed with Buckwheat

Lyeshch Farshirovannyi Keshyei

Although this recipe calls for bream, any sizeable and firm fish may be used. If buckwheat is too bothersome to deal with, use rice in the same quantity.

1.4kg (3lb) bream
100g (4oz) uncooked buckwheat,
  yielding roughly 225g (8oz)
1 minced small onion
175ml (6fl oz) sour cream

Breadcrumbs
Chopped fresh dill
1–2 sliced hard-boiled eggs
Salt
Olive oil

Put the buckwheat into a pan with 1½ times as much water, the onion and salt to taste. Simmer until tender, add a little olive oil and put into an oven to dry. The grains should be separate, as with rice. (If using rice instead of buckwheat, cook it in the same manner.)

Stuff the buckwheat into the fish and arrange it in a shallow baking dish. Pour over it the sour cream and sprinkle with fine breadcrumbs. Bake at 190°C/375°F/Gas 5, basting from time to time. Serve in a hot dish and garnish with hard-boiled eggs, plus any of the filling which is left. Shape the left over stuffing into small balls and put these in the pan with the fish some 10 minutes or so before the fish is ready.

Carp

Sazan or Carp

This fresh-water fish is a favourite in Russia, Poland and the Baltic countries generally, especially as a Christmas dish.

Carp is not a fish with a long history. Larousse says it probably came from China. It appeared in British waters in 1614, left us for Holland and finally migrated to the colder northern waters. My Victorian cook book says of carp: 'It is a pond fish rather than a river fish and required a thoroughly good sauce to be served with it. It is not often offered for sale but it is useful for families residing in the country as it can be obtained when no other fish can be.

'The best carp are of medium size. They are kept a day before they are used. From May to November they are not good for food. The head is considered the best part. Owing to their habit of burying themselves in the mud, the flesh of these fish often has a disagreeable, muddy taste. In cleansing them, therefore, care should be taken to remove the gills as they are always muddy, rub them in salt down the backbone and lay them in strong salt water for a couple of hours. Then wash them in clear spring water.'

Russian cook books list a number of ways in which to cook carp. The scales can be removed, or not; some cooks maintain that carp cooked complete with scales has a better flavour than one which has been carefully scaled.

Carp roe is excellent and is often used in the making of fish balls. Male fish roe is considered to be better flavoured than the female roe. The male carp has a slender shape, while the female delights in feminine curves.

RUSSIAN cooking

Carp Cooked Jewish Fashion

Karp Po-yevryeiskii

1 carp weighing around 1.4kg (3lb)	1 small, sliced onion
300ml (1/2 pint) white wine, water or fish stock	25g (1oz) butter, cut into slices
	175g (6oz) long-grained rice
Salt and pepper	50g (2oz) button mushrooms

Garnish

2 anchovy fillets   1 tablespoon tomato purée

Clean the fish and place it in an oval baking dish. Pour the wine over it, adding enough water or fish stock to come halfway up the sides of the fish. Over the top sprinkle salt and pepper, the onion and butter. Bake at 190°C/375°F/Gas 5 until the fish is tender, about 30 to 45 minutes. Baste it fairly frequently.

While the fish is baking, cook the rice in 900ml (1 1/2 pints) of rapidly boiling, salted water. Let it boil for 5 minutes, then add the mushrooms. Continue cooking until the rice is tender. Drain off the liquid, cover the pan tightly and leave it on the side of the stove to keep hot.

Take the fish from the pan and arrange it on a hot serving plate. Stir the anchovies and the tomato purée together and then into the fish and reheat. Surround the fish with the rice, pour the sauce over it and serve hot.

Usually the carp is arranged in a hoop. If there is too much sauce, take some out before adding the garnish. It can be served separately, or used later to help flavour another fish dish.

Other large, firm fish can be prepared in the same way.

Baked Cod with Mushrooms

Tryeska Zapyechyennaya S Gribami

900g (2lb) cod, cut into steaks
Salt and pepper
1 bay leaf
Chopped carrot and celery, a
  small quantity of both
Breadcrumbs

Olive oil for frying
1 medium-sized, sliced onion
100g (4oz) sliced mushrooms
300ml (1/2 pint) white sauce
Chopped fresh parsley or dill

Cook the fish in a minimum of water, adding salt, pepper, bay leaf, carrot and celery. When the fish is tender, take it from the liquid; remove bones and coarsely flake the flesh.

Heat a small quantity of oil in a frying pan, or small saucepan, add the onion and when this is almost cooked, add the mushrooms; continue simmering for a few minutes.

Put the flaked fish into a shallow casserole, add the mushrooms and onions, cover with the white sauce and sprinkle with breadcrumbs. Bake at 190°C/375°F/Gas 5 for about 20 minutes, or until the fish is reheated and the top of the sauce begins to brown.

To make a more substantial dish add a layer of thickly sliced, cooked potatoes at the bottom of the dish.

Serve sprinkled with chopped parsley or dill.

Instead of white sauce, sour cream may be used; also grated Cheddar cheese mixed with the breadcrumbs.

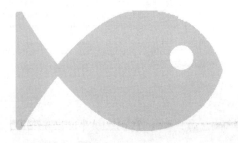

RUSSIAN cooking

Crayfish in Tomato Sauce

Rakovyye Shyeiki V Tomatnom Sousye

Ideally (although it is not often possible) crayfish and other shellfish are best bought fresh and cooked at home.

12 crayfish
Chopped celery, carrot,
  parsnip and parsley
1 tablespoon each black
  pepper and salt

1 coarsely chopped onion
3 slices lemon

Garnish

50g (2oz) sliced button
  mushrooms
300ml (1/2 pint) tomato sauce
  (see pages 196–7)

Dry white wine to taste
Chopped fresh parsley
Lemon juice

Put into a large pan 1 1/2 litres (2 pints) of water, add the vegetables, pepper and salt. simmer for about 30 minutes. In the last 5 minutes, add the lemon. Strain. Return to the pan, add 2.3 litres (4 pints) of water, bring this to the boil and drop in the crayfish. Cook for 5 to 10 minutes, or until they are red. Drain and leave until cool enough to handle. Pick off the shell and remove the black intestinal vein which runs down the centre of the back.

Arrange the crayfish in an ovenproof serving dish. Add the mushrooms. Mix the wine into the tomato sauce, pour this over the fish, sprinkle with lemon juice, dill and parsley and bake at 190°C/375°F/Gas 5 until reheated.

The tomato sauce may also be prepared by simply adding tomato purée to white sauce.

Baked Fresh Herrings

Zapyechyennaya Svyezhaya Syel'd'

Quantities in this recipe are as required.

Rub herring fillets with salt and lemon juice and sprinkle them with finely chopped fresh parsley. Roll up as for roll mops. Rub with olive oil and arrange in a greased baking tin, packing them tightly. Bake at 190°C/375°F/Gas 5 until they begin to brown on the edges.

Serve with mashed potatoes, flavoured with horseradish.

Herrings and Potato Pie

Forshmak Iz Sel'di I Kartofyelya

2 salted herrings	300ml (1/2 pint) sour cream
700g (1 1/2lb) potatoes	Pepper and salt
1 small white loaf (minus crust)	Finely chopped fresh parsley and dill
1 very large cooking apple	Butter for frying
1 large onion	Milk
2 beaten eggs	Breadcrumbs

Soak the herrings in milk for several hours, or overnight. Next day remove the skin and bones and coarsely chop the flesh. Soak the bread in milk. Peel and cook the potatoes in salted water until soft, then mash them until smooth. Peel and grate the apple and finely chop the onion.

Melt a little butter and lightly fry the onion until soft but not brown. Mix this with the herrings. Squeeze the milk from the bread. Add the bread to the herring mixture. Combine this with the apple, potatoes, pepper, dill, parsley, cream and eggs. Pile this into a greased pie dish, sprinkle lightly with breadcrumbs and bake at 190°C/375°F/Gas 5 for about 30 minutes.

RUSSIAN cooking

Oysters in 'Baskets'
(Vol-au-vent Cases)

Ustritsy V Korzinochkakh Ili Volovanakh V Sousye

12 oysters, tinned or fresh	*Vol-au-vent cases (hot)*
200g (7oz) tin crab or fresh crab	*Butter*
Sliced button mushrooms to taste	*Pepper*
Tomato purée	*Dry white wine*

How many vol-au-vent cases are required depends on their size and how many oysters per person served.

Take the oysters and drop them with their liquid into a saucepan, add the crab meat, a little dry white wine, a knob of butter, a few mushrooms, some tomato purée and pepper. bring all this very slowly to the boil, fill the vol-au-vent cases with the mixture and arrange on a serving dish.

Perch

Okun' Morskoy

Perch is a member of a large family of spiny-finned fish who prefer still waters. A bright looking fish, its vertical dark bars are very conspicuous from above. Known as the 'dandy of the stream', when in full condition the perch seems to be well aware of this complimentary title.

From a culinary (and expense) point of view the perch is considered by many to come directly after the salmon and trout. It should be cooked as soon as possible after being caught, and enthusiastic fishermen take a charcoal stove along with them when on a perch catching expedition.

Although the following recipe is meant for perch, the same method of cooking can also be used when dealing with more ordinary types of fish. Most of the Russian recipes actually call for sea perch, which is our bass.

Fish
Ryba

Perch in Sour Cream

Okun' Morskoy Pod Syetannym Sousom

1.4kg (3lb) perch
150ml (1/4 pint) fish stock
  or water

300ml (1/2 pint) sour cream
Flour and vegetable oil
Salt and pepper

Garnish

Sliced fried mushrooms
Sliced spring onions
Potatoes, boiled, sliced
  and sautéed

Hard-boiled eggs
Chopped fresh dill and parsley
Grated Cheddar cheese

Clean the fish and slice it into serving portions. Season a little flour and rub this into the fish. Heat enough oil to fry the fish slices lightly on both sides; take the fish from the pan and arrange in a shallow baking dish. Keep hot.

In the same pan stir in about 25g (1oz) of flour (enough to make a sauce), add the stock and, when blended, add the sour cream. Cook this for a few minutes, until the flour has lost its odour. Pour this sauce over the fish and bake at 190°C/375°F/Gas 5 for about 10 minutes.

In the meantime prepare the garnish. The quantity of each ingredient depends on taste. Any kind of mushroom may be used. Before serving sprinkle the fish lightly with cheese, and garnish.

Stuffed Pike (Or Other Fish)

Shchuka Farshirovannaya

The pike is a freshwater fish found particularly in northern waters. The usual colour of the pike is a pale olive grey, the colour deeper on the back, and marked on the sides by yellowish-white spots or patches. The mouth is furnished with a prodigious number of teeth which is why it is known as the 'Water Wolf', 'Lord of the Stream', and the 'Fresh water Shark'.

It is a highly prolific fish and its multiplication in northern Russia and Siberia is terrific. Salted and dried pike is an important item of Russian export.

RUSSIAN cooking

Formerly it was a much consumed fish in Britain. One pike (size not mentioned) was considered to have 'equal food value with 2 lambs'.

6 thick pike steaks
  (or other fish)
About 100g (4oz) bread
2–3 peeled and chopped onions
Milk
Butter
Salt and pepper
1 lightly beaten egg

25g (1oz) plain flour
600ml (1 pint) fish stock
  or water
2–3 large sliced carrots
2 cooked beetroots, peeled
  and sliced
Chopped fresh dill and parsley
Lemon juice

If using a whole fish, clean, scale and cut into slices about 1cm (1/2in) thick. Lay these in cold water for about 30 minutes. Wipe very dry and rub with salt and pepper, then cut out the centre of each slice without damaging the skin. Sprinkle with lemon juice and leave aside while you prepare the stuffing. Soak the bread in water or milk.

Stuffing

Chop the cut out pieces of fish, mix with the onion, and put through a mincer. Squeeze the bread dry, but not too dry, add this to the minced fish and onion, add salt, pepper and a walnut-size knob of butter and put once more through the mincer. Add the egg to bind the mixture.

Fill the slices of fish with the stuffing, smooth it down with a wet knife. Arrange a layer of vegetables in the bottom of a saucepan, add a layer of fish slices, then another layer of vegetables; a repeat of the fish and lastly one of vegetables. Add enough water to cover and cook slowly (with the lid on) for about 1 1/2 hours.

Take the fish out of the saucepan and lay it on a hot platter. Surround with the vegetables. Put in the oven to keep warm. Make a sauce.

Drain the liquid from the pan, at least 600ml (1 pint). Heat 225g (1oz) of butter, blend in the flour and gradually stir in the fish stock. When the sauce is thick and properly cooked, i.e. when there is no longer the smell of flour, or it has a slightly nutty odour, pour it over the fish. Serve hot with plain boiled potatoes.

Fish
Ryba

Salmon

Lososina

Clean the salmon and cut into thick slices. Put it into a fish kettle and cover with a mixture of half water and half dry white wine. Bring once to the boil, cover and simmer until the salmon is tender.

Serve with butter, either solid or melted, and vegetables to taste.

Soused Smelts

Snyetki V Marinadye

The smelt is a delicately flavoured little fish, less esteemed in Britain today than in Russia. When smelts are absolutely fresh they are said to possess 'a perfume which resembles that of a violet or of a freshly cut cucumber'. However, these resemblances disappear after the smelt is 12 hours out of the water. Then it smells like fish and I must confess that I have never encountered it smelling of anything else.

Smelt can be served alone, or as a garnish. Fresh smelts are very firm, and are of a fine silvery colour, perfumed or not.

48 smelts	*1 bay leaf, 1 clove and 6 peppercorns*
Olive oil for frying	*1 tablespoon finely chopped carrot*
900ml (1 1/2 pints) vinegar	*Salt and pepper*
1 chopped onion	*Milk*
1 stick finely chopped celery	

Clean the smelts, trim off the fins and soak them for a while in milk. Dry carefully, sprinkle with salt and pepper and fry them in hot oil until they are crisp. Drain and arrange in a casserole.

Put the remaining ingredients into a saucepan and bring slowly to the boil. Remove from the heat and leave until cool. When the mixture is lukewarm, pour it over the smelts and leave in a cool place for 24 hours before serving.

Soused smelts are often served as a *zakuski* dish, or as a main dish with hot, boiled potatoes which have been sprinkled with finely chopped fresh dill. Herrings and mackerel can be prepared in exactly the same manner.

Tomato purée is sometimes added to the marinade and the carrot is optional.

Baked Sturgeon

Zapyechyennaya Osyetrina

The sturgeon is a big fish covered with rows of bony spikes and resembling the shark in shape. It is caught in abundance in northern waters and in some parts of the United States, but only very occasionally in British waters, where it is considered a 'royal fish'.

The flesh of the sturgeon has a veal-like texture 'like fish, flesh and fowl', according to whether the flesh is near the skin or the backbone.

Once it was esteemed such an elegant fish that it was crowned before being brought to the table, while a band preceded the table servers as they carried the sturgeon on a platter.

The roe of the sturgeon supplies caviar. And from the sterlet, a kind of small sturgeon, comes the finest caviar, once reserved for the Russian Court.

Not only does the sturgeon produce caviar but also a fish gelatine, visigo, much used in Russian cooking. This is obtained from the spinal marrow and is a rather gooey substance.

It might, in view of what I have written, seem foolish to give a recipe for the cooking of a sturgeon. But a Russian cooking book without a sturgeon recipe would be like a British national cook book without steak and kidney pie.

900g (2lb) sturgeon (or pike, roach, etc.)	1 tablespoon plain flour
25g (1oz) butter	Dry white wine
600ml (1 pint) single cream	Salt

Remove the skin, either scald the fish several times or stand it in salt and water or in a marinade for some hours, then the skin is easily removed.

An hour before the fish is required, rub it with salt, handling it gently but firmly. Moisten it with a little wine, lay it in a dish and put in a hot oven (230°C/450°F/Gas 8). Melt the butter in a saucepan, stir in the flour, gradually add the milk or cream, stirring all the while. Pour some of this sauce over the fish, return to the oven, then from time to time add more until it becomes a golden brown and a light crust is formed. When the fish is tender, take it from the pan and serve with boiled potatoes, garnished with chopped fresh parsley.

Trout Cooked in White Wine

Forel' V Sousye Byeloye Vino

In this recipe the trout should be placed on the grid of a fish kettle so it does not come into direct contact with the liquid. If you do not possess a fish kettle, improvise in a saucepan.

The liquid is a court-bouillon (see below) and, as it is poured into the pan, it should be poured over the fish (i.e. rinsing it), and should reach to just below the top of the grid. Cook over a good heat for around 30 minutes, then lower the heat and continue cooking only as long as the trout required further cooking.

Remove the trout from the pan and carefully skin. Serve garnished with boiled potatoes cut into small balls and lightly fried. Sprinkle with finely chopped fresh parsley and dill.

The trout may be served with a Hollandaise sauce or melted butter.

Court-bouillon

Take 1 part of vinegar, 1 part of dry white wine and 4 parts of water. Put into a saucepan and for every 3.4 litres (6 pints) of liquid allow 15g (1/2oz) of pepper, 25g (1oz) of salt, a bunch of savoury herbs, 2 bay leaves, 1 sliced onion and 1 sliced carrot. Simmer for 1 hour, strain the liquid and it will be ready for use.

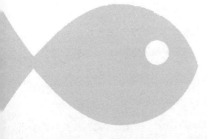

Trout with Walnut Sauce (Georgian)

Forel' V Sousye 'Satsyebyeli'

900g–1.4kg (2–3lb) trout, or
  sufficient for 4 persons
Salt
Wine vinegar

Chopped onions
Radishes
Chopped fresh parsley

Sauce

225g (8oz) shelled and chopped
  walnuts
8–9 tablespoons wine vinegar
15g (½oz) chopped garlic
100g (4oz) minced onion

2 tablespoons finely chopped
  fresh mint
Cayenne pepper and salt to
  taste
Clear fish stock

Clean the trout carefully and wipe dry. Put the fish into water which has been salted and flavoured with 3 tablespoons of wine vinegar to each 1.2 litres (2 pints) of water. Cook the trout until tender and it begins to take on a bluish tinge. Cool and arrange on a plate. Garnish with spring onions, radishes and chopped parsley.

   Prepare and serve the sauce separately. (For many people the above quantity of garlic will be too much, so reduce it if you wish.)

   Mix the onion, garlic, salt, pepper and walnuts together and put through a blender. Add the chopped mint, the vinegar and enough stock to make a thick sauce.

Baked Fish

Rybnaya Solyanka (Zapyechyennaya)

700–900g (1 1/2–2lb) fish,
   preferably 3 kinds
2 shredded braised cabbages
1–2 large, finely chopped onions
1 tablespoon tomato purée
Butter
Pickled mushrooms
Olives, black and green

2 salted, sliced cucumbers
Chopped fresh dill and parsley
2 bay leaves
1 tablespoon capers
Grated Cheddar cheese
Breadcrumbs
Lemon slices as a garnish

Clean the fish, cut off the heads and tails, fillet and cut into portions, 3 to 4 per person. Use the bones, head and tails, skin, etc, to make a stock and into this put salt, pepper, 1 chopped onion and bay leaf. Strain.

Melt 40g (1 1/2oz) of butter and lightly fry remaining onion, add the tomato purée and simmer. Stir in about 300ml (1/2 pint) of the fish stock, bring to the boil, add the fish, cucumbers, pickled mushrooms, remaining bayleaf, capers, and finally the olives. Simmer for 10 to 15 minutes.

Grease a casserole, add half the cabbage, then the fish with its sauce and cover with the remaining cabbage. Sprinkle with mixed breadcrumbs and cheese, dot with slivers of butter and bake at 190°C/375°F/Gas 5 for 10 to 15 minutes.

Serve garnished with sliced lemon, chopped dill and parsley, marinated fruits if available, peeled and salted cucumbers. The usual proportion of olives is more black than green. Instead of braised cabbage, sauerkraut or boiled cabbage may be used.

The fish can be of any type but must be of a firm texture.

Fish in Aspic

Ryba Zalivnaya

1 whole fish, about 900g (2lb)	*1 bay leaf*
1 sliced carrot, onion and leek	*Salt and pepper*
1 stick chopped celery	*1 tablespoon lemon juice*
150ml (¼ pint) dry white wine	*25g (1oz) gelatine*

Garnish

Partly boiled, sliced carrot	*Capers and olives*
Sliced, unpeeled, fresh cucumber	*Chopped fresh dill and parsley sprigs*
Sliced hard-boiled eggs	*Sliced lemon*

Clean the fish and put it (whole) into a pan, with the vegetables, bay leaf, lemon juice, salt and pepper and enough water to more than cover the whole. Cook over a moderate heat until the fish is tender. Take the fish from the pan, put it aside until it is cold.

Strain the stock, return it to the pan and continue cooking until it has reduced to 600ml (1 pint). Dissolve the gelatine in cold water, stir this into the stock, bring to the boil, add the wine, simmer for a few minutes. Leave until cool. Pour a little of the aspic on to a serving plate.

Skin the fish, remove its head, tail and fins, etc, and then cut into thick slices. Arrange these on the top of the aspic in the serving plate. On each slice of fish place a piece of carrot, egg and cucumber. Pour the rest of the aspic over the top, and leave until it jells. When the aspic is quite set, decorate the fish with remainder of the garnish, if available also add some chopped lobster or crab meat.

Serve with a mustard or horseradish sauce, or with mayonnaise.

Marinated Fish

Ryba Marinovannaya

1.4kg (3lb) fish	3 bay leaves
2–3 tablespoons plain flour	6–7 peppercorns
200ml (7fl oz) vegetable oil	salt to taste
600ml (1 pint) wine vinegar	

Bone and skin the fish and wash it well in salt water. Dry, roll in flour, and fry in very hot oil.

Bring the vinegar to the boil, together with the bayleaves, peppercorns and salt. Let this cool and then pour over the fried fish. Keep in a cold place for several hours before using.

Almost any firm fish may be marinated in the above manner.

Fish Piquant

Ryba V Ostrom Sousye

900g (2lb) firm white fish	2 medium, finely chopped onions
225g (8oz) fresh salmon	2 pickled diced cucumbers
1.2 litres (2 pints) cold water,	6 green and 6 black olives
or court-bouillon (page 61)	Lemon wedges
1 bay leaf	Sprigs fresh parsley or chopped
1 teaspoon salt	fresh dill

Poach the white fish only in water or in a court-bouillon for about 20 minutes, adding the bayleaf and salt after it begins to boil. When the fish is tender take it from the pan. Strain off the liquid. Flake the fish and return this to the pan; add half the liquid, slowly bring to the boil, then add to the salmon. Chop the olives (discard the stones), add these to the fish. Simmer until the salmon is cooked. Strain, serve garnished with onions and cucumber with lemon and parsley or chopped dill.

If 2 salted cucumbers are too much, reduce to taste. This also applies to the onions.

Fish Cakes

Bitki Iz Ryby

450g (1lb) filleted fish
2 slices white bread
Milk
2 well-beaten eggs
50g (2oz) butter

Button mushrooms to taste
150ml (1/4 pint) dry white wine
Fish stock or water
Salt and pepper
Breadcrumbs

Clean the fish, remove any skin and chop finely. Soak the bread in a very little milk, squeeze out excess liquid. Mix the fish and the bread, add salt and pepper and put through a mincer or blender. Mix with half the beaten egg and shape into cakes, rather flat. Dip these into the rest of the egg, roll in breadcrumbs and arrange in a large, shallow saucepan. In the spaces between the fish cakes, put the mushrooms, these can be sliced or chopped, as desired. Pour in enough fish stock, or water to prevent burning and cover. Cook very slowly for 20 to 30 minutes.

Take the fish cakes from the pan with a fish slice, cover, or top with the mushrooms, and pour the sauce round them, if there is too much of this, serve some of it in a sauceboat.

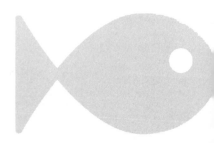

Poultry and Game
Domashnyaya Ptitsa I Dich

With a wide choice of game in many parts of Russia, and some good quality poultry, it is not surprising that there are so many excellent recipes for dealing with both. Most of these are unusual, but what also attracted me was that so many are particularly useful when dealing with young and tender birds.

Chicken Kiev, a favourite recipe of mine, caused me some research. I was curious to discover how it began, for although it is considered essentially Russian, it would appear to be of French origin. I asked several Russian friends, none had the answer. Eventually I was supplied with an explanation which is probably correct.

Chicken Kiev were probably created by one of the French chefs who worked in one of the Russian great houses known for their excellence.

Stuffed Capon (Turkey)

Farshirovannyi Kaplun

1 turkey, prepared for roasting
  about 1.8–2.7kg (4–6lb)
225g (8oz) shelled walnuts
225g (8oz) liver
Madeira
Butter or oil for roasting

2–3 tablespoons soft breadcrumbs
  soaked in a little milk
Salt and pepper
2 beaten egg yolks
25g (1oz) butter

Soak the liver in milk for several hours, or overnight. Blanch the walnuts, peel and chop finely or, better still, put through a grinder.

Drain the liver, chop it and lightly fry with the walnuts, breadcrumbs, salt and pepper, 25g (1oz) of butter and the egg yolks. Stuff this mixture into the bird (neck and rear end) and sew up the openings, or fix with skewers. Rub the bird with butter (use with any surplus from cooking the liver) and put into a baking dish. 'Add a good amount of butter,' the recipe adds. Cover and bake at 190°C/375°F/Gas 5 until tender.

Just before serving add 125ml (4fl oz) of Madeira.

RUSSIAN cooking

Chicken Kiev Cutlets

Kotlyety Po-kiyevski

2 small roasting chickens about
  900 g–1.4kg (2–3lb), or
  4 chicken breasts
100g (4oz) soft white
  breadcrumbs

2 beaten eggs
Salt and cayenne pepper
50g (2oz) butter, frozen hard
Oil for frying
25g (1oz) melted butter

If using whole chickens, some skill is required when cutting them up as only
the breasts are used. The rest of the chicken can be cooked another time.

Blanch the chickens in boiling water for a short while, remove the legs
and wings, then carefully strip off the flesh with a sharp-pointed knife from
both sides of the breast bone. Divide each piece of breast in half, then skin
them carefully. Brush each breast with melted butter and put in the centre of
each piece a knob of frozen butter. Sprinkle with salt and pepper, wrap the
pieces (each separately) round the butter and make each into a hollow cutlet
the size and shape of a carrot. Seal firmly to keep the knob of butter intact
by overlapping the sides, and put the cutlets into a refrigerator for 2 hours.
Spread the breadcrumbs out, or have them in a bowl. Dip the cutlets first
into beaten egg, then into breadcrumbs. Repeat this process. Return them to
the refrigerator and leave for around 30 minutes, or long enough to allow
the coating to set.

Have ready a pan of deep, smoking oil and fry the cutlets for 5 minutes.
Make slits in each portion before serving and warn the family or guests of the
danger of the butter squelching out, as it does sometimes with some force.

Serve the Kiev cutlets very hot with grated potatoes and peas, and garnish
with sprigs of fresh parsley (or watercress) and wedges of lemon. Instead of
putting simple frozen butter into each cutlet, a smaller amount of butter may
be mixed with salt, pepper, chopped fresh parsley and chopped yolk of hard-
boiled eggs, or, if feeling extravagant, with pâté de foie gras and truffle.

The above quantity serves 4 people, that is, one side of a breast for each
person; or 8 if each chicken side is large enough to divide into 2. It depends
entirely on the size of the chickens, and of appetites.

Chicken Cutlets *(Polish Origin)*

Kotlyety Pozharskiye

450g (1lb) chicken
2 slices white bread
Milk
Soft white breadcrumbs

Salt, pepper and pinch nutmeg
25g (1oz) melted butter
Butter or oil for frying

Soak the sliced bread in milk, then squeeze it until fairly dry. Put the chicken through a mincer. Mix these 2 ingredients together, put again through the mincer. Add salt, pepper, nutmeg and the melted butter. Shape into cutlets. Roll in breadcrumbs and fry in very hot butter, or oil, until browned, about 5 minutes. Cover and leave over a low heat for another 5 or 6 minutes.

Serve with melted butter.

In some recipes the cutlets are rolled in beaten egg, plain flour and soft breadcrumbs. Instead of using all chicken, a mixture of veal and chicken is often used. The main factor is that the meat must be white.

Roast and Stuffed Chicken

Kuritsa, Farshirovannaya I Zapyechyennaya

Prepare or have the chicken prepared in the usual manner for roasting. Use a chicken of 1.4–1.8kg (3–4lb) in weight. Keep the liver.

Melt a small quantity of butter and lightly fry the liver, then chop. Take out the soft insides from 2 large bread rolls and soak this in a little dry white wine. Chop very finely a fair quantity of fresh parsley, 1 clove of garlic and 225g (8oz) of shelled walnuts. Mix all these ingredients with the liver and the soaked bread. Whisk 1 egg, then beat it into 150ml (1/4 pint) of dry white wine. Add this to the bread mixture and mix thoroughly. Stuff this into the prepared chicken and roast it in plenty of butter, in a deep pan, first at 230°C/450°F/Gas 8 to allow the bird to brown and seal its juices, then lower the heat to 190°C/375°F/Gas 5 and cook until it is tender.

One good way of testing whether a chicken is tender or not is to take hold of its legs; if they move easily, the chicken is ready.

RUSSIAN cooking

Spring Chicken with Aubergine and Tomatoes

Tsyplyenok S Baklazhanami I Pomidorami

1 spring chicken, about
  1.4–1.8kg (3–4lb)
Plain flour
2 aubergines, peeled and sliced
3 tomatoes, peeled and quartered
300ml (1/2 pint) chicken stock

1 tablespoon tomato purée
Dry white wine to taste
Salt and pepper
Chopped fresh dill and parsley
Butter or oil for frying

Clean the chicken and divide it into serving pieces. Coat each piece with flour. Heat enough butter or oil to fry the chicken until a golden brown. Take out the chicken, put aside, but keep hot. Pour off excess fat from the pan, add the stock, enough wine to flavour the sauce, salt, pepper and, finally, the tomato purée. Bring to the boil, lower the heat and cook for 15 minutes.

In another pan, and using the excess fat, fry the tomatoes and slices of aubergine. Arrange the chicken pieces on a serving plate, surround with aubergines and tomatoes and garnish, with dill and parsley. Serve the sauce separately.

Usually the aubergines are sliced in advance, sprinkled generously with salt and left for 2 to 3 hours between 2 plates, the top one weighted down. This releases excess liquid and less fat is required for cooking.

Chicken with Apples

Tsyplyenok S Yablokami

1 chicken, about 1.4–1.8kg (3–4lb)
450g (1lb) apples, fairly
  sharp and crisp
Plain flour

Butter
Dry white wine to taste
300ml (1/2 pint) chicken stock

Clean and cut the chicken into serving pieces and dip these into flour. Melt enough butter lightly to fry the chicken. Add the stock, stir all together, then transfer to a casserole. Peel and slice the apples, cover the chicken, add the white wine. Put the casserole into a moderate oven (190°C/375°F/Gas 5) and continue cooking until the chicken is tender. Serve in the casserole, with salad, peas or beans, rice or potatoes.

Cider or a light beer can be used instead of wine.

Casserole of Chicken
(Georgian style)

Chakhokhbili Iz Kuritsy

1 chicken about 1.8–2.7kg (4–6lb)	About 75g (3oz) butter
225g (8oz) finely chopped onions	1 tablespoon wine vinegar
2–3 tablespoons tomato purée	Salt and peppercorns
150ml (1/4 pint) chicken stock,	1 bay leaf
or water	
125ml (4fl oz) Madeira (optional)	

Garnish

Tomatoes, lemon and fresh watercress

Clean and cut the chicken into serving pieces. Melt the butter and quickly brown the chicken pieces. Take these from the pan and put into a hot casserole. Fry the onions until they become pinky-brown, then add the tomato purée, stock (or water) and continue cooking until the onions are soft. Pour this mixture over the chicken, add the vinegar, Madeira, bayleaf, salt and peppercorns. Cover tightly and cook slowly either in an oven (150°C/300°F/Gas 2) or on the top of the stove, until the chicken is tender. If a little more liquid is required add either chicken stock or water.

Serve with boiled long-grain rice, garnished with fried tomatoes and thick slices of lemon.

A similar dish can be made with mutton or lamb.

RUSSIAN cooking

Chicken Casserole (Sour)

Solyanka Iz Kuritsy

1 chicken, about 900g–1.4kg (2–3lb)	1 bay leaf
Butter for frying	150ml (1/4 pint) sour cream
2 finely chopped onions	Peppercorns
2 tablespoons tomato purée	1 teaspoon capers
100g (4oz) pickled cucumbers	2 small, sliced gherkins
Chicken stock or water	Black and green olives
	Salt

Dilute the tomato purée with a little of the stock, or water. Clean and cut the chicken into 4 pieces. Melt enough butter to fry the pieces until a golden brown, then add the onions and the tomato purée and simmer gently until the onions are soft. Add the peppercorns, cucumbers, bay leaf and capers. Bring to the boil, add enough liquid to cover, reheat, and cook slowly until the chicken is tender. Just before serving, add the sour cream, the sliced gherkins, a little salt and the olives.

To the above ingredients may be added chopped celery or celeriac.

Duck with Cherries (Roast)

Utka S Vishnyami

1 duck, prepared for roasting, about 1.4–1.8kg (3–4lb)	225ml (8fl oz) boiling water
125ml (4fl oz) Madeira	Chicken stock
	225g (8oz) stoned cherries

Place the duck on its back in a deep roasting pan. Pour the boiling water over it, then put the pan into a hot oven. Turn the duck from time to time and baste frequently in its own liquid. When it is tender, take it from the pan and carve into serving pieces. Keep hot.

Add enough stock to cook the cherries. Strain, add the Madeira, the cherries and, as they begin to soften, the pieces of duck. Cook gently until the cherries are soft. Arrange the pieces of duck on a serving plate, garnish with the cherries. Serve with peas, creamed potatoes and the sauce separately.

If preferred, the sauce can be thickened.

Add salt and pepper if the stock is not already sufficiently seasoned.

Duck with Apples (Roast)

Zharyenaya Utka S Yablokami

1 duck, prepared for roasting, about 1.4–1.8kg (3–4lb)	Little butter
900g (2lb) cooking apples	Sugar

Roast the duck in any manner preferred. Peel, core and cut the apples into medium-thick slices. Arrange these in layers in a baking dish and sprinkle each layer with sugar. Add a little butter and bake at 190°C/375°F/Gas 5 until tender.

Carve the duck, arrange on a serving plate and garnish with apples. Make a gravy from the drippings of duck and pour this over the duck and the apples.

There is a special, rather hard, little green apple which has a short season in Moscow and is much coveted for this particular dish. Usually they are simply peeled and baked whole.

Goose Stuffed with Sauerkraut

Gus' Farshirovannyi

1 small goose, about 1.4–1.8kg (3–4lb)	600ml (1 pint) chicken stock or water
450g (1lb) sauerkraut	Butter
1 large sharp apple	Salt to taste
1 large, finely chopped onion	Caraway seeds to taste

Prepare the goose for roasting in the usual manner and pierce breast all over with a sharp fork to release excess fat. Wash and dry it, rub inside and out with salt. Sprinkle with caraway seeds.

Melt a little butter, slowly fry the onion and when this softens and begins to change colour, add the sauerkraut and chopped apple. Stir these ingredients together and stew gently until the sauerkraut begins to dry out, then add the stock. Cover and continue cooking until the sauerkraut is soft. Stuff this mixture into the goose and sew up. Brush the flesh with butter and place it in a roasting pan. Put into a very hot oven (230°C/450°F/Gas 8) and let it roast at this heat for 15 minutes, then lower the heat to 150°C/300°F/Gas 2 and continue cooking until the bird is tender, a fork should pierce breast meat without too much pressure when done; between 2 to 3 hours' roasting according to the size of the bird.

Incidentally do not overstuff, as stuffing expands with the heat. Another hint, not necessarily Russian, is to let the bird cool slightly before attempting to carve as the joints will then separate more easily.

Partridge with Orange and Grapes

Kuropatka S Apel'sinami I Vinogradom

1 partridge
Butter for frying

1 orange
Handful seedless grapes

Prepare the partridge for cooking (if not already prepared by the butcher) and fry in butter until brown. Put it into a deep dish. Peel the orange and finely chop the rind. Pour boiling water over the rind and immediately drain it. Thinly slice the orange and spread over the partridge. Add the grapes, the butter from the frying pan, sprinkle with orange rind and bake at 190°C/375°F/Gas 5 until tender. Serve the partridge in the dish in which it has been cooked.

Failing grapes, use very light seedless raisins or sultanas.

Pheasant with Apples

Fazn S Yablokami

Pheasant requires to be hung more than any other game bird. According to British lore, it should be hung for as long as possible. The Russians consider 3 or 4 days enough for its flesh to acquire a pleasant flavour and become tender.

Pheasant(s)	Strained chicken stock or water
Streaky bacon	Plain flour
Melted butter	Baked apples to garnish
Blackcurrant jelly to taste	

Rub the bird(s) lightly with salt and wrap in thin slices of streaky bacon. Tie with cotton or fix with minute skewers or cocktail sticks.

Roll the pheasant(s) in flour and place in a roasting pan with plenty of melted butter. Bake at 240°C/475°F/Gas 9 to sear, basting at least twice as the pheasant is a dry bird. Lower the heat to 190°C/375°F/Gas 5 and continue roasting until the flesh is tender and a golden brown. Take from the pan and if the birds are large, halve them, but keep the bacon slices intact. Put aside, but keep hot. Add enough stock (or water) and the blackcurrant jelly to make a fairly liquid sauce. Return the pheasant pieces to this and simmer for another 5 minutes (this is done on top of the stove). Arrange the pieces of bird on a hot, flat dish, garnish with baked apples and the bacon slices. Pour some of the sauce over the pheasant pieces and top with a knob of butter. Serve separately remaining sauce.

Pheasant, Georgian Style

Fazan Po-gruzinski

1 pheasant, plucked, drawn and trussed	50g (2oz) butter
25 shelled and blanched walnuts	Juice 3 oranges
450g (1lb) seedless sultanas	Strong tea

Place the pheasant in a casserole. Add walnuts, sultanas, butter, orange

RUSSIAN cooking

juice and strong tea to cover. Cover with a lid and cook slowly until tender, but beware of over cooking. Serve the pheasant in the sauce. If a darker sauce is required add some brown gravy to it.

Pigeons are also good when cooked in this manner, but formerly the Russians did not eat pigeons as they were considered a holy bird.

See also preceding recipe.

Quail

Pyeryepyel

6 quail
100g (4oz) unsalted butter
 to each quail

150ml (1/4 pint) sour cream

Dress the quail, discard the head and wings, sear and brush with plain flour, then wash in several waters. Dip for 1 second into boiling water. Wipe dry and rub lightly with salt. Tie each quail with string to keep its shape.

Melt the butter to boiling point, clarified butter would be ideal, but it is not essential, in a saucepan. Drop the quails into the boiling butter and fry over a very high heat. Do not cover the pan and take care that the quails do not burn. When evenly browned, take from the pan, remove the string and cut each quail in half.

Put the quail pieces on to a serving plate. Pour off excess butter, leaving only enough to make a sauce. Add the sour cream to the hot butter in the pan, let it come once to the boil, and pour this mixture over the quails.

The quail can also be served whole, they are so tiny.

Braised Hare

Zayats Tushyennyi V Smyetanye

1 hare
Marinade
Streaky bacon
Finely chopped onion

Salt and pepper
Sour cream
Butter or oil

Poultry and Game
Domashnyaya Ptitsa I Dich

There are no exact proportions for this recipe, hares vary in size, so do tastes, and this is the kind of recipe where exactness is not required.

Marinade

Wine and water mixed, enough to cover the hare, 1 tablespoon of vinegar, some coarsely chopped onion, a few slices of carrot, a good handful of chopped fresh parsley and dill, about 6 juniper berries (if available), salt to taste, 6 peppercorns, and 1 tablespoon of sugar.

Cook all this together for about 30 minutes and leave until cool.

The quantity of wine to water can be half and half, or less, or beer or vinegar may be used instead. It depends on taste and availability.

While the marinade is cooling, deal with the hare which, unless it has already been prepared, required skinning, cleaning and cutting into serving pieces. Place these in a casserole, cover with the marinade and leave in a cold place for 24 hours.

Take the hare from the marinade (keep the marinade) and thoroughly dry each piece. Sprinkle with salt and pepper and moisten with sour cream. Wrap each piece in a strip of bacon and tie with cotton. Melt enough butter in a pan to fry the pieces of hare. First fry the chopped onion, then, as this changes colour, add the hare. When a golden brown, put into a deep casserole and cook for a short while, say 5 to 10 minutes, without any liquid.

While this is cooking prepare a sauce.

Strain the marinade and mix this with at least 300ml (1/2 pint) of sour cream. Pour this over the pieces of hare, cover and continue cooking until the hare is tender.

Take the hare from the pan and arrange in a hot dish. Stir a flour and water paste into the sauce to thicken it, it should not be too thick, and pour most of it over the hare pieces. Serve the remainder of the sauce separately.

The usual Russian accompaniment to braised hare is fried potatoes, braised beetroots, boiled beans and semolina dumplings; or creamed potatoes and redcurrant or cranberry jelly.

An old Victorian recipe which I have for a similar English dish concludes with 'a glass of port is always an improvement to hare'. And a Russian-Baltic cooking book suggests a glass of cognac, 125ml (4fl oz), to be added just before the hare is ready.

Braised Hare with Apples

Zayats V Smeyetanye S Yablokami

1 hare cut into serving pieces
Marinade (see page 77)
Streaky bacon
Finely chopped onions
Salt and pepper

Sour cream
Butter
Apples, peeled, chopped
  or sliced

Follow the previous recipe up to the point of cooking the hare until it is tender. About 10 minutes before it is ready, cover with the apples and continue cooking until these are soft.

Instead of fresh apples, dried apples previously soaked until soft may be used.

Serve the pieces of hare with the apples as a garnish. To 1 hare, roughly 450g (1lb) of apples is sufficient.

Rabbit with Prunes

Krolik, Tushyennyi S Chyernoslivom

1 rabbit, prepared for cooking
Melted butter
Marinade (see page 77)
225g (8oz) prunes, soaked and
  drained

Strained chicken stock
Blackcurrant jelly (or
  redcurrant or cranberry)
25g (1oz) each flour and butter

Disjoint the rabbit, put it into a bowl and pour over it the marinade. Leave for 24 hours in a cool place. Take it from the marinade, wipe the pieces dry, lightly fry in hot butter and stir in a little stock and the marinade. Add the prunes half way through the cooking time. When the rabbit is tender, take it and the prunes from the pan and put aside, but keep hot. Melt the butter, add the flour and stir in enough of the liquid to make a thick sauce. Flavour with the fruit jelly. Return the rabbit pieces to the pan, bring once more slowly to the boil.

Serve the rabbit on a hot plate surrounded by boiled long-grain rice. Pour the sauce over the rabbit.

It was surprising to discover several recipes for rabbit in a Soviet cooking book for, before the revolution, no one in Russia would eat rabbit, or so I have been told by an excellent authority.

Wild Boar

Kaban

As wild boar is extinct in Great Britain, there seems little sense in giving any detailed recipe for its cooking.

It is an excellent meat but finest of all is the flesh of the young boar, less than a year old. Boar meat is treated rather like pork but it is usually much leaner and therefore more fat must be used in its roasting than with pork. It should be rubbed with salt and pepper, wrapped neatly in rashers of fat or streaky bacon, and flavoured with juniper berries which will bring out its gamey flavour. It is roasted like pork.

RUSSIAN cooking

Meat
Myaso

It is my experience that those countries which show the most imagination in their cooking of meat, usually do not have meat of the finest quality. Our traditional British roasts are magnificent, but are made so only because of the superb quality of our meat. This was perhaps more evident in the past than it is today, for although superb meat is still available and I suppose always will be, it is often an expensive commodity. When using inferior cuts of meats I heartily recommend some of the Russian methods of cooking them.

A large number of the Russian meat dishes involve cooking in a casserole, either on top of the stove or in a slow oven (150°C/300°F/Gas 2). The secret of these dishes lies in simmering or at least slow cooking, as it does with stews. An interesting and I think unusual feature of many of these dishes is the combination of meat and fruit, the latter usually dried in the form of apricots or prunes, as well as an extensive use of raisins, grapes, sultanas and a wild plum which is grown extensively in Georgia.

Sausages and preserved meats are popular, many heavily spiced, some laced with garlic. A well-stocked Gastronom (delicatessen store in Russia) can boast many different kinds of sausages and preserved meats.

Probably the best known of the Russian meat dishes apart, of course, from the internationally famed Beef Stroganov, is shashlik, which is an early, primitive form of cooking and as much a part of Turkish, Greek and Arab cooking as Russian.

The Georgian word 'shashlyk' means 'food', coming via another Georgian word, 'm'tswade', which is another word for 'meat'. It is a peasant form of cooking, developed from roving tribes and shepherds who lived and roamed among the Caucasian mountains. When they were hungry, they hunted game, speared it with their swords and roasted it over glowing coals. It was a natural method of cooking. From time to time, as a dietary change, they would take a lamb or sheep, it seems that in those days no one minded in the least the occasional loss of such an animal since sheep and lambs abounded on those formidable mountain slopes.

Later the spits were make of oak and there was a saying that 'until a man is old enough to trim the grilling stick with three strokes of the knife, he is not fit to marry'. Chicken livers and birds' tongues, I have read, were spitted on thorns, a tricky business I should have thought, for shepherds' calloused hands. Nowadays every kind of meat is used in preparing shashlyk, including marinaded or fillet of beef, although beef does tend to become dry when grilled like this.

The ancient method of grilling shashlyk was on an open fire, there was no question of finesse. One was hungry, one roasted, one ate. Through the ages, grilling has developed, via human and canine turnspits, to today's streamlined gas or electric grill, as well as the modern charcoal grills which, for the man who likes 'messing about', are to be recommended. If the meat burns a trifle, using any method, this is to the good, since those early shashlyk were also very often burnt. While waiting for the shashlyk to grill, nibble at some *zakuski* and drink vodka or a similar fairly fiery drink. It all helps the atmosphere, if nothing else.

Bacon Cooked in Sour Cream

Svinaya Grudinka V Smyetannom Sousye

This recipe is without any precise quantities.

Thickish slices of raw bacon	Sour cream
Thinly sliced onions	Chopped chives
Salt and pepper	Chopped hard-boiled eggs

Arrange the bacon and onions in a casserole and sprinkle lightly with salt and pepper. Add sufficient sour cream to cover and cook on top of the stove over a low heat until the bacon is tender. Just before serving sprinkle with chopped egg and chives.

Serve with a green salad.

RUSSIAN cooking

Casserole of Beef

Zharkoye

Stewing steak or lamb	Potatoes
Olive oil	Peeled and chopped carrots
Chopped onions	Stock
Peeled and chopped tomatoes	Salt and pepper
Chopped celery	

Clean the meat and cut it into cubes. Heat the oil and fry the onions, add the meat and quickly brown. Add salt and pepper, carrots, celery, potatoes and tomatoes, cover with stock and cook at 150°C/300°F/Gas 2 for several hours.

As with all such dishes, ingredients are as required. They can be omitted or changed as taste and season dictates, especially the potatoes, the casserole is rich and filling enough without them. When stock is not available, use water.

Serve with braised cabbage.

Beef Stroganov (Fillet Beef)

Byefstroganov I

This internationally famed method of cooking fillet of beef is supposed to have been the invention of a Russian general named Stroganov. The Stroganov family, I have read, originates from an adventurer by the name of Josak Jamak who 'conquered Siberia for his family'. They became rich and powerful industrialists with mines in the Urals and neighbouring areas. Ivan the Great granted them fabulous privileges and monopolies until they became 'lords of all they surveyed'. It is perhaps ironic that this once so powerful family should be mainly remembered for a single general (and this may only be legend) who reputedly invented a dish of chopped beef.

700g (1 1/2lb) fillet beef
300ml (1/2 pint) sour cream
6 tablespoons clear beef stock
1 finely chopped onion

50–75g (2–3oz) butter
Salt and pepper
Plain flour

Cut the beef into thin slices and pound gently. Cut again, this time into strips. Sprinkle with salt and pepper and roll lightly in flour. Melt the butter, add the strips of meat and brown. Take from the pan but keep hot. In the same pan fry the onion. Return the meat to the pan, add the sour cream and the stock. Cook, covered, over a very low heat for about 15 to 20 minutes.

If desired, 10 to 12 chopped mushrooms may be added with the onion. There is also a 'Stroganov' made from pork (see page 93).

Beef Stroganov, Ukranian-style

Byefstroganov II

700g (1 1/2lb) fillet beef
1 large, finely chopped onion
Garlic to taste
50g (2oz) butter
25g (1oz) plain flour
125ml (4fl oz) beef stock

100g (4oz) tinned white mushrooms
300ml (1/2 pint) sour cream (not
 yoghurt)
Salt and pepper
150ml (1/4 pint) red wine

Flake the meat with a very sharp knife and put into a basin with the wine, a little chopped onion and garlic. Keep for 2 hours in a cold place. Drain. Keep the wine. Melt the butter and fry the remaining onion, then add the meat. Fry this quickly until brown, sprinkle lightly with flour, salt and pepper and add the stock. Stir until the sauce is thick and a light brown. Add the mushrooms, the wine (which has been saved) and the sour cream. Cover the pan and cook gently for 20 minutes.

RUSSIAN cooking

Beef Grilled on Skewers
(Caucasian)

Basturma

Beef, preferably fillet
Chopped onion
Black pepper
Salt

Dry white wine or wine vinegar
1 bay leaf
Melted butter

Clean the meat, pound lightly and cut it into cubes. Put into a bowl, add chopped onion, salt and black pepper, wine just to cover, and bayleaf. Mix well and leave in a bowl for 3 to 4 hours, covered and in a cool place. Drain and thread the meat on skewers. Grill, preferably over charcoal, turning the skewers frequently to cook on all sides, basting from time to time with melted butter.

To serve, slip the meat off the skewers and garnish with spring onions, sliced tomato and wedges of lemon, or slices of white onion which have been sprinkled with salt, black pepper and vinegar.

One recipe suggested marinating for 3 to 4 days, but not with fillet of beef. Garnish with sliced tomatoes, chopped spring onions and lemon.

Beef with Quinces

Govyadina S Aivoy

450g (1lb) beef, preferably fillet
225g (8oz) quinces
1 minced onion, fried separately

50g (2oz) butter
Salt and pepper
Chopped fresh dill or parsley

Wash the meat thoroughly and wipe dry. Cut into cubes, 3 to 4 per person. Melt the butter in a shallow saucepan and lightly brown the meat. Add water just to cover and simmer for about 40 minutes, longer if not using fillet.

Peel, core and slice the quinces; add to the pan, add the onion, salt and pepper and continue cooking until tender.

Served sprinkled with chopped dill and parsley.

Beef Rissoles
(Russian-style Hamburgers)

Bitki I

450g (1lb) lean and tender beef
  or lamb
1 small, finely chopped onion
1 slice white bread
1 beaten egg

Butter for frying
2–3 tablespoons milk or water
Salt and pepper
Fine breadcrumbs

Soak the bread in the milk until very soft. Squeeze out excess moisture, but the bread must not be too dry. Melt a little butter and fry the onion until it is soft. Coarsely mince the meat, then mix it with the bread, onion, salt and pepper. Bind the mixture with the egg, shape into balls, flatten slightly one side, coat in breadcrumbs and fry on both sides over a moderate heat in a little butter until a golden brown, 8 to 10 minutes.

Bitki are served with a sour cream, or red sauce like tomato sauce, or Madeira sauce, garnished with fried onions and sautéed potatoes. Some recipes call for finely chopped fresh parsley among the ingredients.

Beef Rissoles with Beetroot and Salted Cucumbers

Bitki II

450g (1lb) raw beef or lamb
225g (8oz) cooked beetroot
1 pickled cucumber

1 raw egg
Salt and pepper
Butter for frying

Put the meat, beetroot and cucumber through a mincer. Add salt, pepper and the egg. Shape into rounds. Heat enough butter to fry these until brown on both sides, not deep fat frying.

Serve with tomato sauce, or sour cream sauce, or red, or even Madeira sauce.

RUSSIAN cooking

Beef Rissoles, Moldavian Style

Bitki Po-moldavski

450g (1lb) minced beef or lamb
1–2 tablespoons tomato purée
2–3 tablespoons red wine
1 carrot
1 minced onion
50g (2oz) butter for frying
1–2 egg yolks to bind the
  meat balls

Celery to taste
Parsnip to taste
Salt, pepper and crushed
  garlic to taste
600ml (1 pint) beef stock
1 tablespoon vinegar
Plain flour

Melt half the butter and slowly cook the onion; add salt, pepper and garlic. Take from the pan and mix this with the beef. Add the egg(s), shape the mixture into as many small balls as required, roll in flour and arrange in a casserole.

Peel and dice the carrot, parsnip and celery. Melt the remaining butter and simmer the vegetables until they begin to brown. Add the tomato purée, stock, vinegar, salt and pepper and cook on a slow heat until the vegetables are very soft. Add the wine. Pour this sauce over the meat balls and cook either at 190°C/365°F/Gas 5 or over a moderate heat for about 20 minutes.

Serve with chopped fresh parsley, fried potatoes and sliced, pickled cucumbers.

Stuffed Beef Rolls

Zrazy

12 thin slices of tender beef
1 finely chopped onion
Chopped mushrooms to taste
3 slices stale black bread

Strained beef stock
Salt and pepper
Butter for frying
Chopped fresh parsley or dill

There are many and varying recipes for making zrazy, this one is similar to our own 'Beef Olives'.

Crumble the bread until very fine and soak in a small quantity of strained stock. Pound the meat slices until pliable but not broken. Sprinkle each slice with salt and pepper, and put aside.

Melt a little butter and lightly fry the onion and the mushrooms and finally the breadcrumbs. Add salt and pepper (if required), the parsley and the dill. Take this mixture from the pan and mix well. Put a small portion of this on to each slice of meat, roll up and wrap (without knotting) with fine string or cotton.

Melt some more butter and fry the rolls until brown, then add some strained stock, lower the heat and cook the rolls until tender. Do not add too much stock, the rolls require just enough in which to cook.

Serve with long-grain rice and with a sour cream sauce (see pages 202–3)

RUSSIAN cooking

Beef and Pork Stuffed Cabbage Leaves

Golubtsy, Farshirovannyye Myasom I

1 firm cabbage, weighing
  approximately 900g (2lb)
450g (1lb) ground beef or lamb
225g (8oz) ground pork
100g (4oz) long-grain rice

Salt and pepper
300ml (1/2 pint) milk
25g (1oz) brown sugar
Vegetable oil for frying
Hot water

Cook the rice in milk until soft. Remove the cabbage leaves very carefully so that they remain unbroken. Immerse them in boiling water until pliable. Spread them out and remove the thick centre vein. Join the centre together again, by overlapping the edges.

Mix the meat with the rice, add salt and pepper, then spoon a little of this mixture on to each cabbage leaf. Roll up and fix securely with cotton. Do not tie the cotton in a knot, simply roll it round and round the leaf. It is easier to remove, and this should be done before serving.

Heat enough oil in a large shallow pan to fry the rolls until just brown. Transfer them to a large saucepan, packing them rather tightly together. Sprinkle with brown sugar and add enough hot water to cover the bottom of the pan. You may need to add more liquid as the rolls cook. Simmer for about 2 hours. Serve with a sour cream and tomato sauce.

Sometimes the cabbage rolls are served on slices of crisply fried, rather fat bacon, the sauce poured over them, and sprinkled with chopped fresh parsley, or dill.

Sauce

50g (2oz) butter
25g (1oz) plain flour
2 tablespoons tomato purée

2–3 tablespoons sour cream
Vegetable stock or water

Melt the butter, stir in the flour, add the tomato purée and enough stock, or water, to make a rather thin sauce. Add the sour cream and cook over a low heat until the cream is hot but not boiled. Serve the sauce poured over the cabbage rolls. Or omit the brown sugar and water and, instead, cook the

rolls in the sauce. Both methods of cooking *Golubtsy* are used in Russia.
Golubtsy means 'little pigeons'.

Stuffed Cabbage Leaves

Golubtsy, Farshirovannyye Myasom II

450g (1lb) chopped beef or lamb	50ml (2fl oz) lemon juice
100g (4oz) uncooked long-grain rice	25–50g (1–2oz) brown sugar
1 whole beaten egg	2 tablespoons tomato purée
1 finely chopped onion	Salt and pepper
1 grated carrot	300ml (1/2 pint) sour cream
12–16 cabbage leaves	

Combine the chopped meat, rice and egg. Add chopped onion and carrot,
salt and pepper. Blanch cabbage leaves in boiling water for 2 to 3 minutes.
Flatten them out on a table, remove the centre stalk, overlap the centre
again. Place a ball of stuffing in the centre of each leaf. Roll it up, tucking
in the ends securely. Place the rolls close together at the bottom of a
saucepan. Mix the tomato, sugar, and the cream and pour this over the rolls.
Cover tightly, bring to the boil, lower the heat, add the lemon juice, and
simmer for 30 minutes. Baste from time to time. Reduce the heat and simmer
for 20 minutes. Hot water, if required, may be added in small quantities
during the baking period if the sauce dries.

Serves 4 to 6.

If preferred, the rolls can be tied with cotton. Some cooks fry them before
adding the liquid.

RUSSIAN cooking

Lamb Cooked on a Skewer (Georgian)

Shashlyk

There has been much written about this traditional dish, which at one time was elevated in Russia to the tables of nobles, when it was served on flaming swords, or so one reads.

900g (2lb) boneless lamb	6 crushed peppercorns
2 sliced onions	Tomatoes or bread
Chopped fresh parsley	Spring onions, chopped
125ml (4fl oz) white vinegar or lemon juice	Salt and pepper
	Olive oil

Wash the lamb and wipe it dry; then cut into cubes, about 5cm (2in) square. Sprinkle with salt and pepper, drop into a shallow dish, and add some chopped spring onion (using the green part as well), or chives. Add the vinegar, peppercorns and parsley. Put in a cold place and leave for 4 to 6 hours.

Rub a little oil along the skewers. Thread pieces of meat on to each of the skewers, alternating with a slice of onion. At the end of each skewer fix a piece of bread, or a chunk of tomato (this is not absolutely essential but it helps to keep the meat from slipping off). Fix the skewers over hot charcoal and grill as close to the heat as possible, 5 minutes on each side, turning the skewers frequently to brown the meat and basting from time to time with the dripping in the pan.

Serve on the skewers. Garnish with tomatoes, slices of white onion, this is usually sprinkled with black pepper, salt and vinegar, wedges of lemon and or a wild plum sauce (see page 210). In some parts of Russia dried berries are also served with shashlik.

The best meat for this type of cooking is taken from the leg and, if possible, from a milk lamb. In Moscow shashlyk is served with lettuce, chopped onions and fresh parsley. With milk lamb, no marinading is required. The sliced onion used on the skewers can be marinated before using.

Lamb in White Wine Sauce

Chakhokhbili Iz Baraniny

Another recipe in which quantities are a matter of requirement and taste.

Lamb
Butter
Onion, chopped or sliced
Peeled and chopped tomatoes
Lamb stock

Chopped fresh parsley, dill or
 other herbs available
Plain flour
Dry white wine
Salt and pepper

Wash and wipe the lamb and cut into cubes. Sprinkle generously with salt and pepper. Melt enough butter to fry the onion. As this turns colour, add the meat, brown this, add the tomatoes and enough stock to simmer the meat until tender. Take the meat from the pan, arrange on a hot serving dish, garnished with the tomatoes and onion; strain the stock. Melt about 25g (1oz) of butter in the pan, add an equal quantity of flour, stir to a roux, then add the strained stock. Do this gradually, until you have a thick sauce. Stir in white wine to taste. When adding the wine, take the pan from the fire, then return it merely to reheat and add the chopped herbs. Pour this sauce over the meat and serve with boiled long-grain rice.

   The quantity of onion should be twice that of the tomatoes. For an average family 900g–1.4kg (2–3lb) of meat would be required, the quantity of stock required to make the sauce would not be less than 600ml (1 pint).

RUSSIAN cooking

Mutton in a Saffron Sauce

Chikhirtma

900g (2lb) lamb
2 finely chopped onions
25g (1oz) butter
25g (1oz) plain flour
Lamb stock or water
1–2 egg yolks

Good pinch saffron (soaked in
  a little water)
150ml (1/4 pint) wine vinegar
Chopped fresh parsley and dill, for
  garnish
Salt and pepper

Cut the meat into cubes; put into a saucepan, cover with cold water and bring to the boil. Skin off any scum which rises to the top. Take the meat from the pan and strain the stock.

Melt the butter, add the onions, fry until they begin to change colour, sprinkle with flour and continue cooking and stirring until the mixture is brown. Gradually pour in enough stock to produce a medium-thick sauce. Add the lamb, salt and pepper and finally the saffron. Continue to cook this slowly until the meat is tender.

Just before serving, beat the egg yolks until smooth, add a small quantity of the stock, stir this into the pan, bring again to the boil, take the pan from the heat, sprinkle lightly with parsley and dill, cover and leave for a moment or so before serving. Bring the vinegar to the boil and add this immediately before serving.

Simmered Mutton (Ragout)

Pripushchyennaya Baranina

All quantities are as required and to taste.

Lamb
Onion
Little lemon
Sugar, salt and pepper

Ground ginger and cloves
Lamb stock
Chopped fresh parsley

Slice the lamb into medium-thin slices, allowing 2 to 3 slices per person.

Sprinkle with sugar, salt, pepper, ginger and cloves. Put the meat into a casserole and add enough stock to simmer it gently without burning of turning it into a stew or soup. Cover and leave over the slowest possible heat until the meat is tender.

Garnish with parsley and serve with boiled long-grain rice or buckwheat, or any of the noodle family.

Pork Stroganov

Svinina Po-stroganovski

450g (1lb) lean pork
Butter for frying
1 small, chopped onion
Plain flour
1 tablespoon tomato purée

125ml (4fl oz) meat stock
2 tablespoons sour cream
Chopped fresh dill and parsley
Salt

Clean the pork, slice it thinly and beat. Sprinkle with salt. Melt the butter, lightly fry the meat, add the onion and continue frying over a low heat. Sprinkle the meat and onion lightly with flour, blend, add sour cream, tomato purée and stock. Bring to the boil, lower the heat and cook gently until the pork is tender.

Serve with fried or boiled potatoes and dumplings, long-grain rice or buckwheat, and sprinkled with chopped fresh dill and parsley.

For this dish the pork must be of the very best quality.

RUSSIAN cooking

Pork Chops Cooked in Beer

Svinina, Tushyennaya V Pivye

4–6 pork chops
Olive oil for frying
Plain flour
300ml (1/2 pint) beer
300ml (1/2 pint) white sauce
 (see page 195)

Mixture of carrot, onion,
 turnip and parsnip, in all
 about 225g (8oz), cleaned
 and chopped
Salt and peppercorns
Chopped fresh parsley and dill

Wash and trim the chops, lightly beat them, sprinkle with salt and dust in flour. Heat the oil and fry the chops until brown on both sides. Transfer to a shallow, wide saucepan. Add the vegetables, the beer, salt and peppercorns and simmer until the chops are tender.

Just before serving add the sauce, which must be hot and freshly made. Simmer for a few minutes.

Serve with boiled or creamed potatoes, dumplings, macaroni or any of the noodle family.

Instead of all beer, half stock, half beer, may be used, or a dry cider. The vegetables are often fried before being added, but this makes the dish rather too rich.

Pork in Sour Cream

Zapyekanka Svinaya

There are no precise quantities given in this recipe.

Thin slices of raw pork
Thin slices of raw potatoes
Salt and pepper
Grated onion

Caraway seeds
Sour cream
Butter for greasing

Lightly pound the meat but do not break.

Grease a casserole and cover the bottom with a layer of potato slices. Sprinkle with salt, pepper, caraway seeds and onion. Add slices of pork, then another layer of potatoes and flavourings. Repeat these layers 2 or 3 more times, the top layer must be of potatoes, plus salt, pepper, caraway seeds and onion. Pour over the top as much sour cream as will seep down to the bottom and reach just exactly to the top of the last layer of potatoes. Bake at 190°C/375°F/Gas 5 for about 2 hours.

Veal slices can be cooked in a similar manner.

Veal Cutlets

Kotlyety Iz Tyelyatiny

225g (8oz) minced uncooked veal
1 finely chopped onion,
   medium sized
Small quantity stale bread soaked
   in a little milk
2 eggs, yolks and white
   beaten separately

Salt and pepper to taste
Pinch sweet spices
Olive oil
Breadcrumbs

Heat a little oil and lightly fry the onion. Add this to the minced veal. Add to the bread, which has not been squeezed dry, then add salt and pepper, spices and the egg yolks. Mix until all the ingredients are well-blended. Beat the egg whites until stiff, and fold into the mixture, which is meant to be gooey.

Spread breadcrumbs on to a board, or table, take a portion of the mixture (according to the size of cutlets required) and shape this into a round cutlet. Cover with breadcrumbs. Put aside and repeat this procedure until all the mixture is crumbed and in cutlets:

Heat enough oil to fry the cutlets; do this on both sides and also round the sides. Sprinkle with salt and pepper and either fry to the point of being ready to serve 95 per cent and finish off the cooking in a hot oven (230°C/450°F/Gas 8). This latter process helps to dry the cutlets.

This is the basic recipe for this sort of cutlet. Other kinds of meat, including poultry, may be used, and even fish, provided it is of a firm texture and of good flavour.

RUSSIAN cooking

Veal with Prunes (Baltic-Russian)

Tyelyatina Tushyennaya S Chyernoslivom

900g (2lb) veal
2 finely chopped onions
Plain flour
75g (3oz) butter
225g (8oz) prunes

Dry white wine
Salt and pepper
Pinch nutmeg
Grated rind 1/2 lemon

Soak the prunes in water, do not oversoak them or use too much liquid.

Cut the meat into small pieces. Melt the butter, lightly fry the onions, add the meat and brown it. Sprinkle lightly with flour, and when this is a golden brown, pour the mixture into a casserole. Cover with the prunes, and most of the liquid in which they have been soaking, and fill the casserole with white wine. Add salt and pepper, nutmeg and rind. Bake at 150°C/300°F/Gas 2 until the meat is tender.

Serve with peas and rice, potatoes, or plain long-grain boiled rice.

For those who like fruit and meat mixtures dried apricots can be used as well as prunes in this kind of dish.

Beer or a dry cider may be substituted for the wine. A similar recipe uses beef, adding carrot, tomato purée and plenty of coarsely chopped fresh parsley.

Veal Schnitzel in Sour Cream

Shnitsyel' Iz Tyelyatiny V Smyetannom Sousye

Most of us know veal schnitzels (escalopes) as an Austrian speciality. The Russians appear to have adopted this form of cooking and in their cookery books there are several schnitzel recipes, including some made with fillet of beef, lamb, pork and even cabbage leaves.

2 veal escalopes
2–3 tablespoons sour cream

Butter for frying
Salt and pepper

Trim the escalopes and make a few incisions all round the edges, then pound until they are thin, not broken. Sprinkle lightly with salt and pepper. Melt just enough butter to fry them lightly to a golden brown, by which time the meat should be cooked through. Turn and fry on the other side. Take the escalopes from the pan, and put aside but keep hot. Drain surplus butter into the pan. Pour the sour cream into the fat, stir and bring slowly just to the boil. Pour this sauce over the escalopes.

Serve with peas and sautéed potatoes.

Any meat used to make schnitzels must be absolutely of the finest quality. Each piece should be enough for 1 person and almost as large as the plate on which it is served, this is where clever pounding comes in.

Veal and Pork Balls

Tyeftyeli

225g (8oz) lean veal	Milk
100g (4oz) lean pork	Salt, pepper and chopped
1 large onion	fresh parsley
1 large bread roll	Butter for frying
1 beaten egg	Plain flour

Remove the crust from the roll, crumble the soft part and soak this in enough milk to soften it. Squeeze out the excess milk. Chop the meat and onion coarsely and put together through a mincer. Mix the soaked breadcrumbs with the meat and onion, add the egg, salt, pepper and parsley. Blend well and break off small pieces. Shape these into small balls, roll in flour and fry in fat until a golden brown.

Arrange on a hot plate and serve with a hot tomato sauce (see pages 196–7).

Sometimes the sauce is poured over the tyeftyeli while still in the pan and they are simmered for about 15 minutes.

Either way, serve hot with boiled long-grain rice, or buckwheat.

RUSSIAN cooking

Meat 'Solyanka'

Solyanka Myasnaya

The Russian name 'solyanka' comes from the Russian word for salted, and it is not easy to classify these solyanka dishes correctly. Fish *solyanka*, for example, is akin to a chowder, flavoured with pickled cucumbers or sauerkraut. The following recipe could be described either as a stew or as a very thick soup with a sour flavour. The meats used in its preparations are entirely a matter of choice, they may be mixed cooked meats, cut into cubes, or kidneys and Russian-type sausages, which need to be cooked in the stock, with perhaps the addition of cooked ham and veal.

1.2 litres (2 pints) beef or lamb stock
About 350g (12oz) mixed cubed and
  cooked meats
2 chopped onions
2–3 pickled cucumbers
1 tablespoon capers
10 black olives

2 tablespoons tomato purée
Butter for frying the onions
250ml (1/4 pint) sour cream
Few slices lemon
1 bay leaf
Salt and peppercorns
Chopped fresh dill and parsley

Stone the olives, peel and chop up the cucumbers. Melt the butter and lightly fry the onion until it begins to soften, but do not let it change colour. Stir in the tomato purée, and cook gently for 5 to 6 minutes. In the meantime, heat the stock. Add the meat to the stock, with the cucumbers, capers, bayleaf, salt and peppercorns and finally the onions in tomato sauce. Cook this over a moderate heat for about 15 minutes. Just before serving add the sour cream, the olives, slices of lemon, parsley and dill. Serve at once in soup plates.

Kidneys, Russian Style

Pochki Po-Russki

12 kidneys	1–2 pickled and sliced cucumbers
450g (1lb) potatoes	300ml (1/2 pint) hot sauce such as red sauce
1 carrot	150ml (1/4 pint) sour cream
1 onion	1 bay leaf
1 parsnip (optional)	Salt and pepper
75g (3oz) butter	Chopped fresh dill and parsley

Remove the skin and the centre white from the kidneys. Slice thinly crossways and sprinkle with salt and pepper. Melt the butter and lightly fry the kidneys. Transfer to a shallow saucepan, add the sauce and the cream. Keep the butter in the pan.

Peel and slice the potatoes, carrot, onion and parsnip. Fry these in the butter until they begin to change colour. Add to the kidneys. Add the cucumber and bayleaf and simmer in a covered pan until the vegetables and kidneys are tender.

Serve with chopped dill and parsley. The sour cream may be omitted altogether, or fresh single cream substituted.

Creamed potatoes or boiled long-grain rice is the usual accompaniment to this dish. Enough for 6 people.

For kidneys to be tender they must be cooked a short time or, curiously enough, a long time. So, if cooked beyond the short period, they will have to be simmered for at least 2 hours to be brought back to tenderness, but in the process they will have lost their original juiciness.

RUSSIAN cooking

Kidneys in Madeira

Pochki V Madyerye S Shampin'onami

12 kidneys
75g (3oz) butter
Button mushrooms

600ml (1 pint) Madeira and red sauce
  mixed (see pages 210 and 197)
Salt and pepper

Garnish

Chopped fresh parsley

Remove the skin and centre white bit from the kidneys and slice thinly, crosswise. Sprinkle with salt and pepper. Heat the butter, lightly fry the kidneys and when they lose their pinkish colour, add a little of the chopped parsley and the sauce. Cook gently.

Slice the mushrooms and lightly fry them in a little butter. Add these to the pan and continue simmering for a further 10 minutes.

Instead of a mixed Madeira and red sauce, a white or a béchamel sauce flavoured with Madeira may be used (See page 99).

Liver Cooked in Sour Cream

Pyechyenka V Smyetanye

225g (8oz) liver (beef, lamb or pork)
600ml (1 pint) sour cream
Plain flour
150ml (1/4 pint) beef or lamb stock

1 onion, chopped and lightly
  fried
50g (2oz) butter
Salt and pepper

Wash the liver, remove the skin and tubes which run through it. Slice, sprinkle with salt and pepper and roll it in flour. Melt the butter and lightly fry the liver. When it loses its pink colour, take it out of the pan and put into a shallow dish. Add the onion to the pan and when it begins to change colour, spread it over the liver, plus any butter left in the pan. Add the cream and the stock, cover and simmer for 25 minutes. Do not cook too quickly or the liver will be over cooked and will toughen.

Kidneys may be prepared in the same manner.

Liver Grilled on Skewers

Shashlyk Iz Pyechyenki

Liver	Chopped fresh parsley or
Lamb fat	watercress
Salt and pepper	

Clean the liver. Cut into thick slices, the size depends on the skewers but the pieces should not be as large as for lamb shashlik. Sprinkle with salt and pepper. Cut the fat into small pieces. Thread the liver on to skewers, interspersed with pieces of fat. Grill, turning the skewers frequently, and serve hot.

Serve with chopped, raw or spring onions, chopped parsley, or watercress, and grilled or fried halves of tomatoes.

Tongue in Raisin Sauce

Yazyk Pod Sousom S Izyumon

1 ox tongue	25g (1oz) plain flour
1 carrot	75g (3oz) butter
1 parsnip	Lemon juice
1 onion	Salt and peppercorns
100g (4oz) raisins	

Wash, trim and coarsely chop the vegetables. Wash and clean the raisins, and stone them if necessary.

Wash the tongue, put it into a saucepan, add the vegetables, peppercorns and salt and pour boiling water over it, use plenty of water, and cook the tongue over a good heat for 2 to 3 hours. Take it from the pan, wash it in cold water and skin it quickly, slice and arrange on a hot plate. Strain the stock.

When the tongue is almost ready, make the sauce. Melt 50g (2oz) of butter, add the flour and stir until blended. Add enough of the tongue stock to make a thick sauce. Add the raising and cook fairly rapidly for 8 to 10 minutes. Take the sauce from the heat, add lemon juice and the remaining

RUSSIAN cooking

butter. Pour the sauce over the tongue before serving.

Serve with a purée of green peas or with macaroni or other pasta, such as noodles, or with braised cabbage and creamed potatoes.

Ox, veal or pigs' tongues may be used in this dish, but the latter take a shorter time to cook.

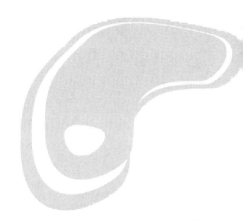

Vegetables
Ovoshchi

'Living in Russia where everything is eaten according to its season is like living in the days of my grandmother,' remarked an American to me, after living for two years in Moscow. 'I had not realized that one should *wait* for vegetables or fruit as they come to the market. Now I have learned the enjoyment to be found in waiting for the cherry season, or for those lovely little green apples which we get in Moscow, and I understand the eagerness with which Muscovites attack the first little green cucumbers, they are so sweet and crisp after the dearth of fresh vegetables in the winter. Came the spring, I really hungered for them myself.'

Taking an overall picture of fruit and vegetables in Russia one finds there is everything, for Russia is vast and its areas embrace hot, temperate and cold climates. In the northern and temperate climate, vegetables are roughly as we have them in Britain, potatoes in masses; beetroots; carrots, both a red and yellow variety; radishes, black, and red and white; cabbage in all its varieties, white, green and, of course, red or purple, red is a misnomer for this brilliantly purple and delicious vegetable.

There are wonderful cucumbers, some short and fat and as round as a tomato, others deeply ridged; some long like the everyday British cucumbers; others almost with the flavour of a fruit. There are large and exceedingly juicy tomatoes, and vast quantities of spring onions, the flavour of which the Russians are unable to resist.

Most of the Russian vegetable dishes are a course in themselves and reasonably simple to prepare and to serve. Cabbage soup, as prepared by the Russian cook or the skilful peasant, is a rich, odorous, succulent dish, fit for prince or peasant.

RUSSIAN cooking

Aubergine in Sour Cream

Baklazhany V Smyetannom Sousye

450g (1lb) aubergines (roughly
  2 large ones)
Oil for frying
Plain flour

Salt and pepper
600ml (1 pint) sour cream
  or yoghurt
Chopped fresh parsley or dill

Wash the aubergines, remove the green tops and, without peeling, slice them in fairly thick slices. Drop the slices into cold, salted water and leave for 5 minutes. Drain and dry. Season enough flour to coat the slices lightly.

Heat about 600ml (1 pint) of oil and fry the coated aubergine slices until brown and crisp. As they become brown, transfer them to a shallow saucepan. When all the slices are in the pan, add salt and pepper to taste to the sour cream and pour this over the aubergine. Bring slowly to the boil, then simmer for 20 to 30 minutes. Serve hot, sprinkled with chopped fresh dill or parsley.

This is a dish for aubergine lovers only. The original recipe called for butter and not oil, but fried aubergines use a lot of fat.

Beans Cooked in Sour Cream

Fasol' V Smyetanye

450g (1lb) green beans
1–2 chopped hard-boiled eggs
150ml (¼ pint) sour cream

25g (1oz) butter
Salt, pepper and chopped fresh dill
Milk or water

Top and tail the beans and break into pieces. Cook in milk or in a minimum of water until just tender. Drain into a colander and pour off any remaining liquid. Melt the butter (in the same pan), return the beans and add salt, pepper and sour cream. Toss and add the eggs and dill. Serve at once.

Beetroot

Svyekla

Wash as many beetroots as required, brush them thoroughly and cook either in boiling, salted water, or bake whole in the oven, until tender. When they are cool enough to handle, discard the skins, chop rather coarsely and gently cook in butter for about 10 minutes. Sprinkle lightly with sugar, salt and the juice of 1/2 lemon. Stir and then pour over them enough fresh single cream to make a sauce. Continue to cook in the cream for another 10 minutes, stirring frequently.

Serve with meat dishes.

Beetroot in Dill Sauce

Svyekla B Sousye S Ukropom

450g (1lb) beetroots	300ml (1/2oz) plain flour
25g (1oz) sugar	150ml (1/4 pint) sour cream
1 tablespoon vinegar	Salt and pepper
25g (1oz) butter	

Peel the cooked beetroots, chop them finely and mash with a fork. Put into a saucepan, add the sugar, vinegar, salt and pepper and slowly bring to the boil. While this is cooking, melt the butter, stir in the flour and, when well-blended, stir this into the beetroots. Add the sour cream, stir again, reheat and serve hot.

Serve with pork chops or ham. Enough for 3 to 4 people.

Failing sour cream, use yoghurt.

RUSSIAN cooking

Cabbage I

Kapusta I

Wash a medium-sized cabbage, removing the damaged outer leaves, and cut into 4 pieces. Discard the thick core and shred the remaining cabbage. Pour boiling water over it (or bring it once to the boil) and leave the cabbage in the water for 20 minutes to soften it. Drain carefully.

Melt 25–50g (1–2oz) butter in a saucepan and lightly fry 1 small finely chopped onion. When it begins to change colour, add the cabbage and cook until it is soft and almost a golden colour.

Cabbage II

Kapusta II

Cut a medium-sized cabbage into 4 pieces and cook in a little water until tender. Drain off unnecessary liquid, put some butter in a pan and, when this is melted, pour it over the cooked cabbage. Sprinkle with fine brown breadcrumbs. The quantity of butter is to taste. (A dish of Polish origin.)

Cabbage III

Kapusta III

1 firm, white, finely shredded
  cabbage
50–75g (2–3oz) butter
1 large minced onion

125ml (4fl oz) thick tomato
  juice
1 tablespoon sugar
Salt and pepper

Melt the butter, add the onion and fry very lightly. Add the cabbage, fry for a few minutes, turning the cabbage over and over so that it is all coated with butter. Add the tomato juice, salt, pepper and sugar; stir well, cover and cook very slowly for 30 minutes.

Carrot Rissoles

Kotlyety Iz Morkovi

450g (1lb) carrots
25g (1oz) semolina
150ml (1/4 pint) cream
Knob butter
2 beaten egg yolks

Salt and pepper
Well-beaten whole egg
Breadcrumbs
Oil for frying

Scrape the carrots, chop and cook in very little salted water until soft. Strain and mash the carrots to a pulp and add the butter. Return to the pan, stir in the semolina, add the cream, 2 egg yolks, salt and pepper. Stir, and when the semolina is cooked and the mixture dry, let it cool. Shape the mixture into rissoles, roll in egg and breadcrumbs and fry in hot oil until brown on both sides.

Serve with a sour cream sauce (see pages 202–3).

Instead of semolina you can use soft breadcrumbs, or cooked long-grain rice. The above quantity makes between 10 to 12 rissoles, according to the size required.

Braised Cucumbers

Tushyennyye Ogurtsy

2–3 medium-sized cucumbers
1 large, finely chopped onion
50g (2oz) butter
Vegetable stock

Salt, pepper and sugar
1 tablespoon lemon juice
Sour cream (optional)
Chopped fresh parsley and dill

Peel the cucumbers and cut them in halves lengthways. Remove the seeds and then cut the cucumbers into pieces about 7.5cm (3in) in length. Melt the butter and lightly fry the onion, add the cucumber, lightly brown, add enough stock almost to cover, salt, pepper and a pinch of sugar; sprinkle with chopped parsley and dill, add the lemon juice and cook gently for 10 minutes. Just before serving, pour the sour cream over the cucumbers.

Dill is a Russian essential when cooking cucumbers. Instead of sour

RUSSIAN cooking

cream, mix a little flour with fresh single cream and cook it long enough to lose the floury flavour.

Serve with boiled or roast meat, or alone.

Stuffed Cucumbers with Sour Cream

Farshirovannyye Ogurtsy B Smyetanye

2 firm cucumbers
225g (8oz) cooked, minced beef or lamb
3 tablespoons cooked long-grain rice

Salt and pepper
Butter for frying
Chopped fresh parsley and dill

Mix the rice and the meat together, add salt and pepper. Peel the cucumbers very thinly and cut into 7.5cm (3in) lengths. Take out the centre of each piece and fill the cavity with some of the meat and rice mixture. Melt enough butter to fry the cucumbers until brown on both sides, then put them in a greased dish and pour the sour cream over them. Sprinkle with dill and parsley. Bake at 190°C/375°F/Gas 5 for about 30 minutes, or until tender. Serve with boiled long-grain rice.

Note that 1 tablespoon of uncooked rice produces about 3 tablespoons of cooked rice.

Potatoes with a Dill Sauce

Kartofyel'naya Zapyekanka V Byelom Sousye S Ukropom

900g (2lb) potatoes
1 finely chopped onion
600ml (1 pint) milk
50g (2oz) butter

1 1/2 tablespoons plain flour
2–3 tablespoons finely chopped fresh dill
4 tablespoons sour cream
Salt and pepper

Scrub the potatoes and cook them in their skins until soft but still firm. While they are cooking prepare the sauce.

Melt the butter and fry the onion until soft, but not brown; add the flour. Blend well, gradually add the milk and bring to the boil. Add salt and pepper and stir to a thick sauce. Add the dill and finally the sour cream. Simmer.

By this time the potatoes will probably be cooked. Peel and slice them thickly as soon as it is possible to handle them and drop at once into the simmering sauce. Continue cooking slowly for several minutes and serve very hot.

Potatoes Baked in Sour Cream

Kartofyel' Zapyechyennyi V Smyetannom Sousye

900g (2lb) potatoes cooked in their skins
1 medium-sized onion, finely chopped
75g (3oz) grated cheddar cheese
2 whole eggs

Breadcrumbs
25g (1oz) butter
300ml (1/2 pint) sour cream
Salt and pepper

Melt the butter and lightly fry the onion until soft but not brown. Peel and slice the potatoes. Arrange them in layers in an ovenproof dish interspersed with the onion and grated cheese. Sprinkle with breadcrumbs. Whisk the eggs into the sour cream and pour this mixture over the breadcrumbs. Add salt and pepper to taste and bake at 190°C/375°F/Gas 5 until the top is a golden brown.

Serve as a main dish or with roast or boiled meat.

Baked Potato Pie

Kartofyel'naya Zapyekanka

900g (2lb) potatoes
2 large onions
2–3 streaky bacon rashers
Butter

150–300ml (1/4–1/2 pint) sour cream
Plain flour
Salt and pepper

Thinly slice the potatoes. Finely chop the onion and bacon. Grease a casserole.

Arrange a layer of sliced potatoes at the bottom of the casserole, sprinkle with onions, bacon, salt and pepper. Add another layer of potatoes, another of onions, etc, and repeat this until the potatoes and onions are used up.

Sprinkle every other layer with salt and pepper. Mix into the sour cream a little flour, enough to thicken it slightly, and spread this over the top. Bake at 190°C/375°F/Gas 5 until the potatoes are soft.

Instead of sour cream a white sauce may be used, into which an egg yolk had been beaten.

All these potato dishes are served with either roast or boiled meat, or as a main dish. The quantity of sour cream does rather depend on individual taste and availability.

Potato and Herring Pie

Kartofyel'naya Zapyekanka S Syel'dyu

900g (2lb) potatoes	Breadcrumbs
2 salted herrings	Butter
225ml (8fl oz) sour cream	Pepper

Cook the potatoes in their jackets. When cool enough to handle, peel and slice them. Fillet the herrings and cut into small pieces. Grease a casserole with butter.

Arrange a layer of the sliced potatoes on the bottom of the casserole, cover with salted herring, add pepper if desired, another layer of potatoes and herrings and continue until these ingredients are used up. Pour sour cream over the top to make a covering crust, sprinkle lightly with breadcrumbs and bake at 230°C/450°F/Gas 8 until the top is golden brown.

The number of layers depends entirely on the size of the casserole, but generally 3 of potatoes and 2 of herrings is enough. The top layer should be of potatoes.

Sauerkraut Pie with Salted Cucumbers

Solyanka Iz Kvashyenoy Kapusty

900g (2lb) sauerkraut
50g (2oz) butter
1 large onion
1 tablespoon plain flour

2–3 pickled cucumbers
300ml (1/2 pint) vegetable stock
450g (1lb) assorted cold meats
Salt and pepper, if required

Garnish

1/4 sliced, pickled cucumber

Slice the onion and the cucumbers; coarsely chop the meat.

Melt the butter and lightly fry the onion until soft. Add the flour and stir until blended. Gradually add enough stock to make a thickish sauce. Add the sauerkraut and the cucumbers and cook gently until the sauerkraut is soft and dry. Put a layer of this mixture into a dish, add a layer of meat, another of sauerkraut, then of meat and finally finish with sauerkraut. Dot with slivers of butter.

Garnish with sliced, pickled cucumbers (other than those used in the pie).

Salt and pepper can be added if required, but remember the cucumbers have plenty of salt.

Instead of adding slivers of butter, beat up some sour cream or milk, mix it with egg and spread this over the top. Or, instead of sauerkraut use shredded white cabbage and 1 tablespoon of vinegar. Add tomato purée to taste, diluted with the stock and flavoured with 1 teaspoon of sugar.

Failing cold meat, use sliced Frankfurter sausages.

Black olives can also be added as a garnish.

RUSSIAN cooking

Spinach

Shpinat

900g–1.4kg (2–3lb) spinach
50g (2oz) butter
1 small, finely chopped onion

1 chopped hard-boiled egg
Salt and pepper
Nutmeg

Clean the spinach and wash it thoroughly. Shake off the water. Melt the butter in a large saucepan, lightly fry the onion until it is soft but not brown. Add the spinach and without covering the pan cook over a good heat until tender. Add salt and pepper, a good pinch of nutmeg and sprinkle with the hard-boiled egg.

Spinach with Fish (Baked)

Shpinat S Ryboy

Spinach cooked as in preceding
  recipe
Cooked, filleted, coarsely
  chopped fish

Salt and pepper
Grated Cheddar cheese
Milk or single cream
1–2 chopped, hard-boiled eggs

Put the cooked spinach through a mincer, or chop it finely. Mix this with the fish. Grease a pie dish, or casserole and fill with the spinach and fish mixture. Mix enough grated cheese with cream or milk to make a covering. Pour this over the top of the spinach, add finely chopped eggs, salt and pepper and bake at 190°C/375°F/Gas 5 for 20 minutes.

Tomatoes

Pomidory

Choose large, firm tomatoes for this recipe. Drop them into boiling water and leave for a few minutes, or until it is possible to peel off their skins easily. Cut each tomato in half. Lay these in a greased pie dish, sprinkle with finely chopped onion, fresh dill, salt and pepper; top with slivers of butter and bake until soft at 230°C/450°F/Gas 8.

Vegetable Ragout

Ragu Iz Ovoshchyey

The vegetables given in this recipe may be changed according to season.

450g (1lb) potatoes	1 tablespoon plain flour
3 carrots	Salt and pepper
2 turnips	Small piece cinnamon
2 finely chopped onions	2–3 cloves
2 tablespoons tomato purée	Chopped fresh dill and parsley
50g (2oz) butter	

Clean the potatoes, carrots and turnips, peel and cut them into good-sized cubes. Cook in boiling, salted water until tender, but not too soft. Drain off the liquid, put the vegetables into a dish and keep hot. Melt the butter, add the onion and fry this until soft but not brown. Add the flour, blend well into the butter and onion, add the tomato purée, stir well then gradually add enough of the vegetable stock to make a sauce of medium thickness. Return the vegetables to the pan, pour over them the hot sauce, add the cloves and cinnamon, and simmer for 15 minutes, not longer, or they will become mushy. Sprinkle with chopped dill and parsley before serving.

Other suggestions are celery, swedes, cabbage, beans, peas, tomatoes, etc. If using very small onions, either cut them in half or use whole.

RUSSIAN cooking

Vegetable Ragout (Moldavian Style)

Givyech Ku Lyegumye

Aubergines
Courgettes
Carrots
Tomatoes
Onions
Parsnips
Peppers

Peas
Garlic
Clove, bay leaf, cinnamon
Salt and sugar to taste
Butter
Vegetable stock or water to cover

Trim and peel the first 6 vegetables and cut into medium-thick slices. Slice the peppers, remove all the seeds and core. Melt the butter and lightly fry these vegetables. When lightly browned, add stock, peas, garlic, bay leaf, cinnamon, salt, pepper and sugar and continue cooking until all the vegetables are very soft.

Serve as a main dish or with boiled pork, beef, lamb or fish.

This is another recipe in which almost every ingredient can be altered to suit one's taste and the need of the moment, and is reminiscent of ratatouille.

Salads
Salaty I Vinyegryety

If among the recipes given me for this section there had not been old as well as new (some are a couple of hundred years old), I would have declared that there was a strong American influence evident in Russian salads. This thought can be turned round, and it can be said with justice that there is a strong, if not heavy, Russian influence evident in American salads. If one took this chapter out of its present setting and put it straight into an American cooking book, no one would doubt they were all recently invented American salads. I have tried them with success on many people, even the most bizarre of them, or at least those which seem bizarre to the simple lettuce and tomato salad eaters.

Incidentally, what goes under the name of Russian salad in Europe and our own country is vinagrette to the Russians, and there are or were some 100 or more varieties on the basic recipe. One friend of mine remembers that her mother had recipes for 36, and this, she insisted, was not even half of them. Therefore, it must be that almost 'anything goes' for Russian salad.

Beetroot Salad

Salat Iz Svyekly

Cooked beetroots
Oil and vinegar
Salt and pepper
Caraway seeds

Clove
Cinnamon
Thinly sliced lemon or
 orange peel

The flavour of beetroots is much improved if they are baked at 190°C/375°F/Gas 5 until tender, instead of being boiled in water.

Cool the beetroots, add vinegar and oil, salt and pepper, a few caraway seeds, 1 clove, a pinch of cinnamon and lemon or orange peel.

Usually the peel is used in its dried form, but fresh peel, too, has an attractive flavour when used with beetroots.

Cabbage Salad, Red

Salat Iz Kapusty Krasnokochannoy

450g (1lb) red cabbage
2 tablespoons olive oil

125ml (4fl oz) vinegar
1 teaspoon sugar, brown preferred

Clean the cabbage, remove any decayed or broken leaves. Cut into 4 pieces and then cut away the thick stems. Shred the remaining cabbage. If the cabbage is young, garden fresh, it can be used raw, otherwise it must be partially cooked.

Scald the cabbage with boiling water, cover the pan and let it steam for about 20 minutes. Drain, pour cold water over it, then squeeze out all the moisture. Turn into a bowl. Pour vinegar over it (this is to retain its red colour). Add the sugar and the oil and turn it about with a wooden spoon until all the ingredients are blended. Leave for about 30 minutes and serve cold. Serve with meat, game, poultry and fish.

Cabbage Salad, White

Salat Iz Kapusty Belokochannoy I

450g (1lb) crisp white cabbage
150ml (¼ pint) vinegar
 or lemon juice

1 teaspoon sugar
Salt and pepper
1 tablespoon olive oil

In this salad you can use either all white cabbage, or mix with it some red cabbage.

Wash and strip the outer leaves of the cabbage; remove the thicker stalks and shred the remaining leaves. Pour some boiling water over the cabbage, cover and leave for 20 minutes. Drain thoroughly, rinse in cold water, drain well again and arrange in a salad bowl. Mix the oil and vinegar (usual dressing form), add salt, pepper and just a little sugar. Pour this over the cabbage and turn the leaves until all have a little of the dressing. Leave for at least 1 hour before using.

To this salad may be added grated apple which has been mixed with lemon juice and sugar.

Cabbage Salad, White with Apples and Celery

Salat Iz Kapusty Belokochannoy II

450g (1lb) white cabbage	150ml (1/4 pint) vinegar
1–2 stalks celery	1 tablespoon sugar
1 large sharp apple	

Wash and strip off the outer leaves of the cabbage and cut away the thick stalks. Shred the cabbage and stir into it the vinegar and sugar. Peel and chop the apple, clean and chop the celery. Mix into the cabbage and serve at once with fried or roasted hot meats, or cold, sliced meats and fish.

This salad has a sweet and sour flavour.

Sauerkraut Salad (Salted Cabbage)

Salat Iz Kvashyenoy Kapusty

450g (1lb) sauerkraut	Finely chopped onion
1 tablespoon olive oil	Few caraway seeds, if liked
Pepper	

Pour boiling water over the sauerkraut, then squeeze it dry. Add the remaining ingredients, mixing them well into the sauerkraut.

Diced apple, sugar and lemon juice are often added, to taste.

RUSSIAN cooking

Cauliflower Salad

Salat Iz Tsvyetnoy Kapusty Pomidorov I Zyelyeni

1 small, cooked cauliflower
3–4 peeled tomatoes
1/2 medium-sized cucumber
Handful cooked green beans, cut
  into diamonds
2–3 finely chopped spring onions

Few lettuce leaves, broken
  into small pieces
3–4 tablespoon sour cream
3–4 tablespoons mayonnaise
Pinch salt
Salt and pepper to taste

What the Russians mean by 'diamonds' is simply cutting the cooked beans at an angle.

Mix all the vegetables, except the onions, together. Combine the sour cream with the mayonnaise, add salt and pepper, stir this into the vegetables, turn into a shallow salad bowl and garnish with spring onions.

Chopped apples, young turnips and radishes, even seedless grapes, are other possible ingredients.

Salted Cucumber Salad

Salat Iz Solyenykh Ogurtsov

2 pickled cucumbers
1 teaspoon olive oil

1 teaspoon wine vinegar
Few pickling onions

Slice the cucumbers very finely. Mix the oil and vinegar together and add the onions. Combine all ingredients and serve with cold meats.

Potato Salad

Salt Iz Kartofyelya

Boiled potatoes, as required
Spring onions, or chives, to
  flavour

Salad dressing
Salt and pepper

Peel and slice the potatoes. While they are still warm, add the salt, pepper and dressing. Garnish with onions, or chives. Serve cold but not refrigerator cold.
  Old potatoes make a better salad than new.

Potato and Sweetcorn Salad

Salat Iz Kartofyelya I Kukuruzy

450g (1lb) cooked, chopped
  potatoes
175g (6oz) tinned sweetcorn
Spring onions, or chives, to
  flavour

Vinegar and oil dressing
Sugar
Pepper

Cook the sweet corn in boiling, salted water until tender. Cool and mix with the potatoes, add the remaining ingredients, garnish and serve cold.

Radish Salad with Sour Cream

Salat Iz Redisa V Smyetanye

Slice as many radishes as required and mix with sour cream. To this can be added finely chopped chives, fresh dill or parsley, hard-boiled eggs, salt and pepper to taste.
  Fresh cucumbers are treated in exactly the same manner, either sliced or diced. Or mix radishes and cucumbers together.

RUSSIAN cooking

Russian Salad I

Vinyegryet I

Pre-revolution Russian cooks were, I have been told, able to list at least 36 different kinds of *vinyegryet*, which, of course, must account for the astonishing diversity of the salad internationally known as 'Russian Salad'.

Cold cooked carrots	Olive oil and vinegar for marinade
Cold cooked potatoes	Chopped herring fillet
Cold cooked peas	Chopped anchovy fillets
Cold cooked beetroots	Finely chopped fresh dill and parsley
Dressing	

Cut the potatoes, beetroots and carrots into julienne strips and marinate them with the peas in a mixture of oil and vinegar. Strain, add the herring and anchovies and enough dressing to hold the salad. Sprinkle with chopped dill and parsley.

   Instead of herring, shrimps may be used.

Russian Salad II

Vinyegryet II

Remains of cold, cooked meats, cut into thin slices and then into thin strips	Fresh cucumbers or gherkins, cut into thin strips
Cold cooked carrots, cut into thin strips	Hard-boiled eggs, sliced
	Few stoned and chopped olives
Cold cooked potatoes, cut into thin strips	Salad dressing
	Cooked or tinned shellfish

Put the meat, carrots, potatoes and cucumbers into a bowl. Add the dressing, chill, and turn the mixture into a salad bowl. Garnish with slices of hard-boiled eggs, chopped olives, and if available, some cooked prawns, shrimps, or other type of shellfish.

   Instead of the dressing, mayonnaise can be used.

Russian Salad III

Vinyegryet III

Cold cooked carrot, cut
 into julienne strips
Cold cooked beetroot, cut
 into julienne strips
Cold cooked potatoes, cut
 into julienne strips

Sauerkraut
Spring onions
Salad dressing or
 mayonnaise

Pour boiling water over the sauerkraut, then squeeze it dry. Mix the vegetables together, add the dressing, blend thoroughly and leave to stand for 15 minutes to settle.

'Russian' Green Salad

Russki Zyelyenyi Salat

Finely chop raw cabbage, raw spinach, celery, lettuce, green peppers, onions (preferably spring) and fresh cucumbers. (The cucumbers must be finely sliced, sprinkled with salt, and kept in a separate, not metal, dish for at least 1 hour before adding to the rest of the salad.) The liquid which oozes from the cucumbers should also be added.

Make a salad dressing, i.e. a simple one of oil and vinegar, or a sour cream dressing, but not mayonnaise, and pour this over the ingredients. Slice some firm tomatoes and spread these over the top of the salad. Serve cold.

RUSSIAN cooking

Orlov Salad (Fruit, Vegetable and Meat)

Salat Iz Sye'dyeryeya, Yablok I Oryekhov

There is probably a book to be written on dishes which have made names famous. The Orlov family, an old Russian noble family, has quite a number of recipes attributed to it. One Count Orlov served under Katherine II and later, in 1762, was involved in a palace revolution which cost Peter the Great his life, strangled by the Count. Whether he was the one who invented this salad I do not know. Whoever did invent it left no detailed directions; however, it makes very good sense.

Mix together chopped celery, cold cooked peas, tender, chopped runner beans, cooked flowerettes of cauliflower, a few asparagus tips, cold, cooked strips of chicken breasts, diced lean, cooked ham and tongue, chopped, sour apple and chopped pineapple. Blend together with mayonnaise and sprinkle with chopped, blanched walnuts.

Modern Russian cooking books, scorning titles, list this salad as 'Celery, walnut and apple salad'.

Apple and Carrot Salad
(Baltic-Russian)

Salat Iz Morkovi I Yablok

Equal quantities sour apple and
  carrots, peeled and grated
Horseradish to taste
Salt and sugar

Lemon juice
Sour cream
Olive oil
Vinegar

First prepare the dressing by mixing oil, vinegar, salt, sugar and horseradish and finally sour cream. Mix the apple and carrot and stir the dressing into this.

Fruit Salad with Mayonnaise

Salat Iz Fruktov

3 sour apples
1 firm pear
1 orange
1 tangerine

3 tablespoons mayonnaise
1 tablespoon lemon juice
1 teaspoon icing sugar
Pinch salt

Wash the fruit, peel and slice, remove pips and cores, etc. Put into a mixing bowl, add the sugar, a pinch of salt and then the mayonnaise. Sprinkle with lemon and serve. Garnish with strips of orange or tangerine rind. (Or with grapes, or cold, cooked prunes.)

A similar salad may be prepared with apricots, peaches, stewed quinces or any of the berries. But apples must always be used.

Served with cold roast or boiled meat and game.

Pineapple and Celery Salad

Salat Iz Ananasa S Sel'dyeryeyem

Chopped fresh pineapple and
  celery in equal quantities
Lettuce leaves, as a base

Cooked sliced beetroot, as a garnish
Oil and vinegar dressing

Mix the pineapple with the chopped celery. Add the dressing and garnish with the beetroot.

RUSSIAN cooking

Salad Demidov (Rice and Tomato Salad)

Salat 'Dyemidov'

In quantities to suit individual needs:

Cooked long-grain rice
Chopped tomatoes

Salt and pepper

Garnish

Mayonnaise

Beetroots

Mix the rice, tomatoes and salt and pepper well together, naturally the main ingredients must be rice. To this may be added chopped celery. Cover lightly with mayonnaise and garnish with beetroots, the latter cut into thin slices and halved.

Demidov is another of those Russian names which have come down through the ages, via the cooking books. Like the Stroganovs, they started as a family of important industrialists and in 1720 were created a noble family, for which, my source adds cynically, 'they had to thank their arms factory in the Urals'.

Egg Salad with Sour Cream

Salat So Smyetanoy I Yaitsom

1 lettuce
1 small cucumber
2 hard-boiled eggs

90ml (3fl oz) dressing made from mixing
   sour cream and mild vinegar
Salt and pepper

Clean the lettuce, break it into pieces and line a salad bowl. Slice the eggs, peel and slice the cucumber. Arrange the egg and cucumber slices on the lettuce and add the sour cream dressing.

Serve with cold meat or fish.

Crab Salad

Salat Iz Krabov

200g (7oz) tin crabmeat
1 cooked turnip, diced
1 carrot, diced
2–3 cooked potatoes, diced
1 fresh cucumber, peeled
  and sliced
1 tomato, sliced

4 tablespoons cooked peas, or
  chopped, cooked French beans
1 lettuce
Mayonnaise
1 tablespoon olive or
  groundnut oil
2 tablespoons vinegar

Clean the lettuce and break the leaves. Line a salad bowl. Around the side
of the bowl arrange the vegetables, the diced ones with the peas or beans
in small heaps, the sliced ones as garnish. At the last moment, put the crab
meat, drained free of its liquid, in the centre of the bowl. Keep the liquid.

Immediately before serving, add salt and a dressing made from
mayonnaise, olive oil, vinegar and the liquid from the tinned crab.

Salted Herring Salad

Salat S Sel'd'yu

2 salted herrings
4 chopped, cooked potatoes
1 peeled and chopped apple
2 small sliced cucumbers
1 medium-sized, chopped onion
2 chopped hard-boiled eggs
Chopped, cooked crab (optional)
300ml (1/2 pint) sour cream or
  mayonnaise

Salt and pepper
Vinegar and olive oil (mixed as
  dressing)
Chopped fresh parsley
Capers and pickling onions, as
  garnish
Milk

Clean the herrings and soak for several hours in milk. Take out the bones
and chop the flesh into small pieces.

Into a bowl put the herrings, potatoes, apple, cucumbers, onion and half
of the hard-boiled eggs. Add salt and pepper and dressing to taste. Finally

RUSSIAN cooking

stir in the sour cream, or mayonnaise, garnish with the remaining chopped egg, parsley, capers, onions and crab meat, if used.

Instead of crabmeat, diced cold, cooked meats, including ham, may be used.

Sturgeon Salad

Salat Iz Osyetriny

450g (1lb) boiled and flaked fish
450g (1lb) sliced, cooked potatoes
Sliced gherkins, to taste
1 lettuce
Mayonnaise
2 sliced hard-boiled eggs

Black caviar (optional)
Small quantity crabmeat or
  lobster
Black olives
Smoked salmon
Salt

Make sure there are no bits of skins or bone in the fish. Also that the fish is firm, white and of good flavour. Do not add too much salt.

Tear 2 to 3 lettuce leaves into very small pieces. Put the fish, potatoes, gherkins and broken lettuce leaves, sliced hard-boiled eggs and shellfish into a bowl. Mix with mayonnaise, but not too much.

Just before serving, line a salad bowl with remaining whole lettuce leaves, add the salad and garnish with caviar, black olives and strips of smoked salmon.

Sweet Dishes
Sladkiye Blyuda

'The Russians in my experience do not appear to have any sweet dishes except the inevitable *kisyel* and stewed fruit,' remarked a friend who had just returned from a long tour of duty in Russia when she discussed Russian cooking with me in the early days of preparing this book.

But as I delved more and more into the subject I found that, although this might be true as far as the majority of Russian restaurants are concerned, it is not true of Russian cooking generally. I think the following recipes prove this.

Stewed Apples or Pears

Kompot Iz Yablok Ili Iz Grush

900g (2lb) apples or pears
175g (6oz) sugar
150ml (1/4 pint) red wine

25g (1oz) blanched almonds
1 tablespoon lemon juice

Peel the fruit, cut into quarters and discard the core and pips. Put the fruit into a saucepan with cold water to cover, add half the quantity of sugar and the lemon juice. Cook slowly until soft. Take out the fruit and arrange in a bowl. Add the remaining sugar to the juice in the pan, bring to the boil, add red wine and simmer for a couple of minutes. Leave the juice to cool.

Cut the almonds lengthways, toast in a little butter and stick them into the pieces of fruit. Add the juice and serve cold.

Another method of cooking apples or pears is to peel, core and slice them into rings and cook gently in a syrup made from sugar and water. The wine and almost can be omitted, and lemon or orange rind added instead for extra flavouring.

RUSSIAN cooking

Stewed Chestnuts

Kompot Iz Kashtanov

24 large chestnuts
100g (4oz) sugar
300ml (1/2 pint) cold water
Vanilla essence

Thinly sliced lemon or orange
  peel
125ml (4fl oz) sherry
Caster sugar

Cook the chestnuts in salted water for 5 minutes, or until the brown outer and inner skins can easily be removed. Be careful not to break the chestnuts.

    Make a syrup with the sugar and water, add the sherry, vanilla, lemon rind and the chestnuts. Cover and cook gently until tender but not broken or too soft. Serve hot, sprinkled lightly with castor sugar and, if desired, single fresh cream.

    If the chestnuts are not suitable for serving whole, cook them until they are quite soft, strain (keep the liquid) and rub the chestnuts through a sieve. Return to the saucepan and add about 150ml (1/4 pint) of the liquid in which the chestnuts were cooked. Stir, add the same quantity of fresh single cream, bring slowly to the boil, simmer until the cream thickens. Take from the heat, cool, and chill. Serve in glasses, with whipped cream.

Stewed Oranges

Kompot Iz Apel'sinov

6 oranges
225g (8oz) sugar

300ml (1/2 pint) hot water
Orange liqueur

Wipe the oranges and cut (unpeeled) into thin slices. Discard the pips. Boil the water with the sugar to make a syrup, add the oranges and simmer for 15 minutes. Take the slices from the pan, arrange these in a bowl and add the liqueur to the syrup as a flavouring. Pour this over the oranges, cool then chill.

    Or peel the oranges and carefully remove all the pith before slicing. Or mix tangerines with the oranges. Tangerines, however, must be skinned, the pith and pips discarded, and then divided into sections, not sliced.

Dried Fruit Compote (Mixed Fruit)

Kompot Iz Smyesi Sushyenykh Fruktov

100g (4oz) dried apples
100g (4oz) dried pears
100g (4oz) dried figs
100g (4oz) dried apricots

100g (4oz) raisins
450g (1lb) sugar, or to taste
Lemon juice to taste

Sort over the fruit and wash it several times in warm water. Soak overnight in enough water to cover. Next day drain. Put each type of fruit into a separate saucepan, add hot water to cover, add sugar, cover and simmer until the fruit is soft. Cool and finally mix all the fruit together, adding lemon juice to taste.

Another version of this recipe is simpler. All the ingredients are soaked in the same pan overnight. Next morning the liquid is drained off and cooked to a syrup with the sugar and a strip of lemon rind. A little ground cinnamon and nutmeg is added. When the syrup is thick, the fruit is added and cooked very slowly until soft. It is left to cool in the syrup.

Although the recipe advises soaking the fruit overnight, this depends on the quality of the dried fruits. Modern methods of drying fruits have made overnight soaking unnecessary. However, raisins and figs blend better with other fruits if they are soaked for 5 minutes in boiling water. All these fruit increase their bulk when cooked. The compote should be a thick mass of mixed fruits with not too much liquid.

Kissel

Kisyel'

This is a Russian form of soft pudding which the Russians call a jelly, although it is not in fact the kind of jelly we know. It is made from fruit, usually, and thickened with potato flour or cornflour. The former is preferred as it helps to retain the original colour of the fruit.

There are roughly three types of kissel; almost thick enough to cut, served in a 'shape' and with cream, either fresh or sour; semi-stiff, served in the dish in which it was set, with cream or a fruit sauce; and finally the 'runny' kissel,

RUSSIAN cooking

which is really a fruit sauce.

Before pouring the hot kissel into a bowl, first rinse the bowl with cold water and sprinkle it lightly with castor sugar. Also sprinkle the top of the kissel lightly with sugar, to prevent the formation of a skin.

For want of a better translation I have used the anglicized version of the Russian name, *kisyel*.

Apple Kissel

Kisyel' Iz Yablok

900g (2lb) apples	*1 tablespoon lemon juice*
175g (6oz) sugar, or to taste	*2 tablespoons cornflour*

Wash and chop the apples and cook with the lemon juice in 300ml (½ pint) of hot water until very soft. Rub through a sieve. Mix all but about 225ml (8fl oz) of the apple purée with the sugar and return this to the pan. Mix the remainder of the purée with the cornflour, stir this into the pan and bring all to the boil. Simmer for a few minutes, stirring all the time. Pour in a rinsed and sugared bowl, chill and serve with whipped cream.

Cherry Kissel

Kisyel' Iz Vishyen

450g (1lb) morello cherries	*2 tablespoons cornflour*
275g (10oz) sugar	*Little lemon juice*

Wash the cherries, remove the stones and sprinkle the flesh with sugar. Leave for about 40 minutes. Stir several times to release the juice. Pour off this juice and put it aside. Smash the cherry stones, pour 600ml (1 pint) of water over them, bring to the boil and cook for 5 minutes. Strain and pour this liquid over the cherry pulp, add the first lot of cherry juice, a little lemon juice and cook until the cherries are soft. Cool and rub through a sieve. Return to the pan, bring once more to boiling point and add the cornflour (mixed with a little water to make a thin paste) and cook, stirring all the time, for 5 minutes. Pour into a rinsed bowl, chill, and serve with whipped cream.

The cherries used in this recipe must above all be ripe and full of juice. If sweeter cherries than the morello are used, use less sugar.

If the cherries are not juicy, ignore the advice about releasing the juice, the result is still very pleasant.

Gooseberry Kissel

Kisyel' Iz Krizhovnika

700g (1½lb) gooseberries
900ml (1½ pints) water
Small piece lemon rind

175g (6oz) sugar
2 tablespoons cornflour

Wash, top and tail the gooseberries and cook them with the rind in the water until very soft. Rub through a sieve. Add the sugar and bring to the boil. Mix the cornflour with enough water to make a thin paste. Stir this into the gooseberries and bring slowly to the boil and, stirring all the time, cook for 5 minutes. Pour into a bowl, cool, then chill and serve with whipped cream.

For a stiffer kissel use less liquid.

Cranberry Kissel

Kisyel' Iz Klyukvy

450g (1lb) cranberries
600ml (1 pint) water

225g (8oz) sugar, or to taste
50g (2oz) cornflour

Remove the stalks and wash the berries in hot water. Mash to a pulp and pass through a sieve. Put into a saucepan with the sugar and water and bring to the boil. Lower the heat and cook very slowly for 5 minutes.

Mix the cornflour with water to a thin paste. Stir this into the fruit and, stirring continuously, bring to the boil again. Cook for a further 5 minutes. Leave to cool, then chill to set. Serve with cold milk, or fresh cream.

Cranberry kissel is also served hot, with sour cream.

RUSSIAN cooking

Plum Kissel

Kisyel' Iz Sliv

450g (1lb) plums
225g (8oz) sugar, or to taste

2 tablespoons cornflour (mixed
  with water to a thin paste)

Wash the plums, slit them and remove the stones. Put the plums into a saucepan, cover with sugar and leave until a juice runs from them, stirring frequently. In another pan boil the stones for 10 minutes in just over 600ml (1 pint) of liquid. Strain and pour this liquid over the sugared plums. Cook until they are soft. Rub through a sieve; return to the saucepan and bring once more quickly to the boil. Add the cornflour paste, stir and cook for another few minutes. Pour into a rinsed dish, chill and serve with whipped cream. This particular kissel is sufficiently stiff to turn out of its mould.

Mixed Berry Kissel

Kisyel' Iz Klubniki Zyemlyaniki Maliny Yezhyeviki

In more or less equal proportions, in total weighing 450g (1lb), use ripe:

Garden strawberries
Wild strawberries
Raspberries
Blackberries

225g (8oz) sugar
50g (2oz) cornflour
Lemon juice

Wash the fruit in cold water. Put into a pan and cook slowly for a few minutes in just sufficient water to cover. Rub through a sieve, mix with the sugar and add a little lemon juice. Return to the pan and bring slowly to the boil. Take the pan off the stove, remove any scum which might have formed on the top of the fruit. Mix the cornflour with a little water to a thin paste and pour this into the pan. Stir well and bring the fruit gently once more to the boil, stirring all the time. Pour this into a rinsed dish and leave to cool.

Serve chilled, with whipped cream.

Strawberry Kissel

Kisyel' Iz Klubniki Ili Zyemlyaniki

450g (1lb) strawberries, garden or wild   50g (2oz) cornflour
225g (8oz) sugar, or to taste   600ml (1 pint) water

Wash the strawberries and rub through a sieve. Put aside. Put the sugar and water into a pan, bring to the boil and cook to a syrup. Mix the cornflour slowly with enough of the hot syrup to make a thin paste, pour this back into the syrup, bring once to the boil, cook for 1 to 2 minutes, and take the pan from the stove. Pour the syrup into the sieved fruit, stirring all the while and leave to cool.

Can be prepared equally well with raspberries, or other berries.

Almond Kissel

Kisyel' Mindal'nyi

225g (8oz) sweet almonds   1.7 litres (3 pints) water
50g (2oz) bitter almonds   50g (2oz) cornflour
75g (3oz) sugar

Blanch the almonds and grind them as finely as possible. Gradually mix with all but 225ml (8fl oz) of the water. Squeeze through a jelly bag, or a piece of muslin cloth. Rub the pulp which remains through a coarse sieve. Stir back into the almond liquid. Pour into a saucepan, add sugar and bring slowly to the boil. Mix the cornflour with the remaining water to a paste, stir this into the almond liquid and cook gently for 5 minutes. Pour the mixture into rinsed glasses and cool. Chill and serve either with fresh whipped cream, or fruit sauce.

Unusual but very good.

# RUSSIAN cooking

Milk Kissel

Kisyel' Molochnyi

1.2 litres (2 pints) milk
75g (3oz) sugar

3 blanched, chopped bitter almonds
50g (2oz) cornflour

Take enough milk to mix the cornflour into a thin paste. Heat the rest of the milk with the sugar and the almonds, bring slowly to the boil, stir in the cornflour paste and stir until the mixture has thickened. Turn into a dish. Leave to cool and chill in a refrigerator.

This type of kissel must be eaten very cold. Serve with a fruit sauce or whipped cream, or sprinkle it generously with grated nuts. Instead of bitter almonds, almond or vanilla essence, grated lemon or orange peel may be used.

Apple Snow with Gelatine

Sambuk Yablochnyi

900g (2lb) apples
50–75g (2–3oz) sugar

3–4 egg whites
1 level tablespoon dissolved gelatine

Peel and core the apples and bake them in a little water in the oven until very soft. While still hot rub through a sieve and stir in the sugar. Beat the apple purée until the sugar has dissolved. Add the egg whites (one at a time without previous beating) and continue beating until the mixture has become light and fluffy and almost white in colour. Dissolve the gelatine according to the instructions and stir this into the apple. Pile the mixture into small glasses or one glass dish and leave until set.

May be served with whipped cream, small macaroons, wafer biscuits, or 'baby' meringues.

Baked Apple Snow

Vozdushnyi Pirog Iz Yablok

6 large cooking apples   2–3 tablespoons sugar
6 egg whites

Bake the apples whole in a hot oven (250°C/450°F/Gas 5) until soft, then rub through a sieve. Add the sugar and put the mixture into a pan on top of the stove and cook this until it thickens. Beat the whites until a solid froth then whisk the whites and apple purée together (while the purée is still hot). Pile into a soufflé dish, smooth down with a palette knife and bake at 190°C/375°F/Gas 5 until the top is a golden brown. Serve immediately.
    This is a type of soufflé and the literal translation is 'air pie from apples'.

Coffee Cream

Kofyeinyi Zavarnoy Kryem

150ml (1/4 pint) strong coffee   175g (6oz) caster sugar
600ml (1 pint) milk   8 egg yolks

Cream the sugar and eggs, add the coffee and milk. Pour into the top of a double boiler and cook over hot water until the mixture thickens. Pour into individual glasses. Serve with chocolate biscuits, sponge fingers, etc.

Rum Cream

Kryem Romovyi

5 egg yolks   300ml (1/2 pint) single cream
50g (2oz) sugar   225ml (8fl oz) rum
25g (1oz) gelatine

Beat the yolks until thick and gradually add the sugar, beating continuously. Dissolve the gelatine in water. Add a little sugar, then stir it into the eggs. Stir in the cream, and when completely blended, add the rum. Pour into a mould and leave until set.

Honey Mousse

Myedovyi Muss

150ml (1/4 pint) clear honey   4 eggs

Separate the egg whites from the yolks. Beat the yolks until creamy and add the honey. Pour this mixture into the top of a double boiler over hot water and cook until it thickens. Take from the pan. Beat the egg whites to form stiff peaks. Fold into the yolks and honey. Pour into individual dishes and serve cold.

Instead of beaten egg whites, whipped cream may be used, or both.

This recipe was marked by the Soviet cook of a friend as being very popular in Moscow. It is very sweet, but rather pleasant and smooth. The honey tends to fall to the bottom of the glass, leaving a light brown frothy mixture on top.

Egg-nogg

Gogol'-mogol'

175g (6oz) caster sugar   300ml (1/2 pint) rum, brandy or
Grated orange rind to taste   orange liqueur
6 egg yolks

Mix the rind and sugar together. Beat the egg yolks with the sugar and mix until almost white. Add the liquid and beat again. Pour into glasses, chill and serve with a rich biscuit.

For my taste this is too sweet. I use only 100g (4oz) of sugar. I have also cooked the mixture in the top of a double boiler until thick, then chilled it. Both methods are very palatable. Orange Liqueur gives the best flavouring.

Wild Strawberry Jelly

Zhyelye Iz Zyemlyaniki

450g (1lb) wild strawberries
600ml (1 pint) boiling water
225g (8oz) sugar
Strained juice 2 lemons

150ml (1/4 pint) Madeira or
   sweet red wine
25g (1oz) gelatine

Put the berries into a deep earthenware casserole, cover with boiling water and place in a slow oven (150°C/300°F/Gas 2). Leave for several hours, even overnight if necessary, it becomes a thick juice.

Dissolve the gelatine according to the instructions. Strain the strawberry juice through muslin into a saucepan. Add sugar; when this is dissolved bring the juice to the boil. Add the lemon juice, Madeira and dissolved gelatine. Cool and pour into a mould. Leave in a cold place until set. Unmould and serve with sweet biscuits or wafers and thick, or whipped cream.

Raspberries may be treated in the same manner but this jelly is especially good when prepared with wild strawberries.

Red Wine Jelly

Zhyelye S Krasnym Vinom

750ml (1 1/4 pints) red wine
3–4 tablespoons sugar
Lemon rind to taste

7 teaspoons gelatine
225ml (8fl oz) hot water

Garnish

Whipped cream

Dissolve the gelatine in 225ml (8fl oz) of hot, but not boiling water. Add a little sugar and the rest of the water. Let this cool. Bring the wine with the remaining sugar and the lemon rind to the boil, but it must not actually boil. Strain. Mix the gelatine into the wine and pour this into a rinsed mould. Leave in a cold place to set. Unmould and serve with whipped cream.

RUSSIAN cooking

Apple Charlotte with White Bread

Babka Yablocknaya I

1.4kg (3lb) apples
700g (1½lb) sliced white bread
600ml (1 pint) milk
1–2 eggs

75–100g (3–4oz) sugar
Butter
½ teaspoon cinnamon
Lemon juice to taste

Peel and core the apples, and cut into cubes. Put into a saucepan, add a little butter, sugar, cinnamon and lemon juice. Simmer until almost soft. Remove the crusts from the bread, then cut each slice into 2 or 3 pieces.

Generously grease a charlotte mould or a casserole. Beat the egg(s) into the milk. Dip the pieces of bread into this. Line the bottom and sides of the mould with the soaked bread, overlapping the edges so that it fits snugly and the apple does not escape. Leave some bread to cover the top. Pour the cooked apple into the centre of the mould, add the remaining bread, still overlapping it, cover and bake at 190°C/375°F/Gas 5 for about 40 minutes. The bread when ready should be a golden brown colour. Leave for 10 minutes, turn out and serve with an apricot or other fruit sauce, with whipped cream, or with a sugar syrup.

In some recipes it is suggested that the bread be diced and some of it mixed into the apples. But this makes the charlotte rather stodgy, although if the bread is mixed with the apples, rather less apples are required.

Instead of dipping the bread into egg and milk, white wine or sherry may be used. Sometimes the slices of bread are lightly fried in butter before being dipped either in milk or in wine, this I think is quite an improvement.

Apple Charlotte with Brown Bread

Babka Yablochnaya II

1.4kg (3lb) apples
100g (4oz) sugar
About 450g (1lb) black breadcrumbs
  (rye or pumpernickel)
2–3 eggs
350g (12oz) seedless raisins
150ml (1/4 pint) sweet white wine
Butter

Grated rind 1/2 lemon
Grated rind 1/2 orange.
1–2 tablespoons ground almonds
4 tablespoons vegetable oil (or
  peanut oil)
2 cloves
Grated nutmeg

Peel, core and coarsely chop the apples. Cook with the sugar, a little butter and a very little water until almost soft. Mix the breadcrumbs (made from stale bread) with the oil, blend and mix into the apples. Separate the egg yolks from the whites. Beat the yolks until fairly thick, add the wine, raisins, almonds, orange and lemon peel, cloves and a good pinch of nutmeg and mix with the apple. Whip the egg whites until stiff and fold into the mixture. Pour into a well-greased dish (the usual charlotte shape) and bake at 190°C/375°F/Gas 5 for 45 to 50 minutes.

Can be served as it is or with a fruit sauce, preferably according to Russian taste, apricot.

Charlotte Russe

Babka Iz Vzbitykh Slivok

600ml (1 pint) single cream
50–70g (2–3oz) sugar
Clear jelly (preferably red)
15g (1/2oz) gelatine
Vanilla flavouring to taste

3 stiffly beaten egg whites
About 20 sponge fingers
Glacé cherries
Tinned or crystallized apricots
Raspberry purée

Rinse a charlotte mould or soufflé dish in cold water, pour in enough jelly to

RUSSIAN cooking

give a thin lining on the bottom. Let this set. With some of the fruit make a pattern on top of the jelly, cover this with more jelly and again leave until set.

Line the sides of the mould with sponge fingers, standing them on their ends so that they rest on top of the hardened jelly, they should not pierce it. Cut off the tops level with the top of the mould.

Dissolve the gelatine in cold water, adding the sugar. Whisk the cream until stiff and add the gelatine and vanilla. Finally fold in the egg whites. Leave until almost set, then pour into the lined mould. Leave until absolutely stiff, turn out to serve. Garnish with remaining fruit and the purée.

Instead of using vanilla or raspberry purée, sherry, Madeira or a liqueur can be used as a flavouring.

By jelly I do not mean a jam. It may be made from packaged jelly, or a fruit juice set with gelatine. Not much is required.

Coffee Charlotte Russe

Sharlotka Kofyeynaya Zamorozhyennaya

600ml (1 pint) single cream   *100–150g (4–6oz) sugar*
100g (4oz) freshly ground coffee   *25g (1oz) gelatine*
8 egg yolks   *450g (1lb) sponge fingers*

Bring the cream to the boil in a double boiler, add the coffee, stir well, take from the heat and leave for 1 hour. Strain through a fine sieve. Beat the egg yolks until they begin to thicken, add the sugar and continue beating until the mixture is very thick. Add this to the coffee and cream mixture, beating well. Dissolve the gelatine according to the maker's instructions and stir this in. Allow the mixture to cool, and leave until it begins to set.

Cover the bottom of a rinsed charlotte mould (or similar type of dish) with sponge fingers, cutting them to fit snugly and neatly. Line the sides by standing the biscuits on end all round, and very close together. Fill with the mixture, cover with remaining biscuits, and leave in a cold place until the cream is quite set. Trim off the tops of the sponge fingers level with the top of the mould and turn out to serve.

Serve with whipped cream.

Instead of using ground coffee, I have also tried using very strong black prepared coffee and dissolving the gelatine with this instead of water. It wastes no cream since there is no need for the sieving of the cream and coffee grounds together, and I found the mixture rather smoother. But it is essential that the coffee should be both fresh and strong.

A chocolate Charlotte Russe can be made in the same manner. Substitute 75g (3oz) of unsweetened chocolate for the coffee.

Milk Pudding

Bubyerts

900ml (1½ pints) milk
Small piece vanilla, or essence
3 egg yolks
2 tablespoons sugar

3 tablespoons fine white flour
25–50g (1–2oz) chopped almonds
3 stiffly beaten egg whites

Beat the egg yolks and the sugar together until very thick and fluffy, add the flour, blend, then add enough milk to make a medium-thin paste. Bring remainder of the milk to the boil, gradually stir in the milk and egg paste and, stirring continuously, cook for another 5 minutes. Add the almonds, then take the pan from the stove and, still stirring, fold in the egg whites. Leave until cold, chill, and serve with any kind of fruit sauce or with jam.

This is a version of our nursery cornflour pudding, but much lighter and without its often appalling stodginess.

Instead of white flour, semolina may be used.

Wild Strawberry Pie with Shortcrust Pastry

Pyesochnaya Baba S Zyemlyanikoy

Shortcrust pastry for a two crust pie
Wild strawberries
Sugar
25g (1oz) plain flour

600ml (1 pint) sour cream
1 beaten egg yolk
25g (1oz) caster sugar
Fine biscuit crumbs

Line a 23cm (9in) pie dish with pastry.

Wash the strawberries (enough to fill the pie generously) and dry them in

RUSSIAN cooking

a towel. Sprinkle with sugar and biscuit crumbs. Sprinkle the base of the pastry with half of the flour and add the strawberries. Cover with the remaining pastry. Make a hole the size of a penny in the middle. Bake at 230°C/450°F/Gas 8 for 35 to 40 minutes, or until a golden brown.

Mix the cream, egg yolk, sugar and flour together and when the pie is half-cooked, pour this sauce through the opening in the centre of the pie.

Failing wild strawberries, other soft berry fruits may be used.

Plain Batter Pudding

Drachyena I

100g (4oz) plain flour	600ml (1 pint) warmed milk
3 eggs	1/4 teaspoon salt
150ml (1/4 pint) sour cream	Butter to grease the dish

Garnish

Caster sugar   Melted butter

Sift the flour into a basin, make a well in the centre and break in the eggs. Mix thoroughly, add the sour cream and salt and beat the mixture until smooth. Gradually beat the milk into the batter and beat steadily for a few minutes. Pour the batter into a greased baking dish and bake at 220°C/425°F/Gas 7 for 30 minutes. Serve at once sprinkled with castor sugar and plenty of melted butter. Drachyena is also served with lemon juice, fruit sauce and jam.

A Russian friend of mine always adds 3/4 teaspoon of sugar to the *drachyena* mixture, rather as one adds a pinch of salt to a cake mixture. It does not make the pudding sweet but adds something to its flavour.

Rich Batter Pudding

Drachyena II

100g (4oz) flour	Grated rind 1 lemon
2 tablespoons sour cream	1 tablespoon cognac
5 beaten egg yolks	5 stiffly beaten egg whites

Garnish

Strawberry compote, or fruit sauce, or cherry jam

Sift the flour into a bowl and mix with the sour cream to a paste. Add the egg yolks and lemon rind; when completely blended add the cognac and finally fold in the egg whites. Grease a soufflé dish, pour in the mixture and bake at 230°C/450°F/Gas 8 until a golden brown. Turn out to serve.

'Pull' Bonbons

Tyanuchki

Mix in equal quantities single cream with sugar, add vanilla to taste and bring this to the boil. Cook until thick and solid. Stir several times and pour into a plate previously covered with greased kitchen paper. Leave until cold and cut into shapes, squares, diamonds, etc.

These bonbons are sticky or gummy like nougat, hence their name.

Although the recipe does not specify using a double boiler, it is a wise precaution against burning.

RUSSIAN cooking

Buckwheat, Rice and Pasta
Krupyanyye I Muchnyye Blyuda

Buckwheat

Kasha

225g (8oz) buckwheat
600ml (1 pint) water

1 tablespoon olive oil
Salt

Method 1

Wash the buckwheat. Pour the water into a saucepan, add salt and bring to the boil. Add the buckwheat, stir, skim off the grains which come to the top, add the oil, stop stirring and let the buckwheat cook until it becomes thick like a porridge and all the liquid has evaporated. Cover tightly and leave for 3 to 4 hours.

Cooking buckwheat is rather like cooking rice.

Method 2

Grease a large frying-pan, add the buckwheat and, stirring all the time, cook until the grains become a golden brown. Put these into the top of a double boiler and add cold salted water until it covers the top of the grain. Add the oil and cook for 2½ hours. Loosen the grains from time to time with a fork. The grains must be soft, but not soggy, as separate as the rice grains in a pilau.

Kasha is served with melted butter, sugar and milk, as a porridge; or in the many ways of serving rice; or in place of potatoes with the main course at lunch or dinner. It keeps cooked, as long as rice, and what is not eaten today may always be utilized the day after.

It is possible to spoil several lots of buckwheat before the knack of cooking it is learned, in the same way that rice is often spoiled. Buckwheat, like rice, has an unfortunate tendency to become soggy.

Buckwheat Baked Pudding

Gur'yevskaya Kasha

450g (2lb) washed buckwheat
1.2 litres (2 pints) vegetable stock
175g (6oz) chopped mushrooms

Salt and pepper to taste
Olive oil

Cook the buckwheat as in method 1, using stock instead of water, and with the mushrooms. When it is thick, arrange it in a well-greased baking tin. Put into a moderate oven (190°C/375°F/Gas 5) and bake until the top is browned.

Rice may be used instead of buckwheat.

Semolina Dumpling

Mannyye Klyetski

600ml (1 pint) milk
1/2 teaspoon salt
25g (1oz) butter
225g (8oz) semolina
3 egg yolks

75g (3oz) sugar
6 finely chopped, blanched
  almonds
Grated rind 1/2 lemon
Breadcrumbs

Bring the milk, salt and butter to the boil gradually, stirring all the while, then add the semolina and cook this until thick. Leave until cold.

Beat the egg yolks until thick, add the sugar, continue beating until this is dissolved, add the almonds and the lemon rind, and combine this with the cold semolina. Shape into balls, roughly the size of hen's egg, roll these in breadcrumbs and fry in deep oil until a golden brown.

Serve with stewed fruit and or thick fruit juice.

RUSSIAN cooking

Semolina Pudding

Gur'yevskaya Kasha

175g (6oz) semolina
2 beaten eggs
100g (4oz) sugar
600ml (1 pint) milk

50g (2oz) butter
50g (2oz) almonds, lightly roasted
Vanilla flavouring to taste
Tinned fruit to choice

Bring the milk to the boil and add the sugar and vanilla flavouring. (The Russians use vanilla pod, which has a much nicer and softer flavour.) Gradually add the semolina, stirring all the time. Cook over a moderate heat for 10 minutes. Add the butter. Take the pan from the heat, stir in the eggs. Reheat, stirring all the time, and then pour the mixture into a greased dish. Sprinkle with caster sugar and put the dish into a hot oven (250°C/450°F/Gas 8). When a brown skin forms on the top it is ready.

Just before serving garnish with fruit, add the fruit juice and sprinkle with roasted almonds.

This is definitely an Eastern-style dish, and very similar to the Pakistani *sooji halva*. Instead of tinned fruit, crystallized fruit is sometimes used, and walnuts as well as or instead of almonds.

There are several wheat grain puddings of this type, all said to have been named after a man named Guryev.

Semolina Wine Pudding

Puding Iz Mannoy Krupy S Vinom

300ml (1/2 pint) sweet white wine
300ml (1/2 pint) water
100g (4oz) semolina
100g (4oz) sugar

Vanilla essence, to taste
2 beaten egg yolks
3 stiffly beaten egg whites
Butter for greasing

Bring the wine and water to the boil. Stir and add the semolina; take the pan from the heat, add sugar and vanilla and return to the heat and continue stirring until the semolina is thick. Remove from the heat again, gradually beat in the egg yolks, and finally fold in the whites.

Grease a pudding basin, pour in the semolina, cover with greaseproof paper, stand in a pan with water to come half way up the side of the basin, bring to the boil and cook for about 30 minutes. Cool and turn out. Serve with a sour fruit sauce.

Instead of white wine, sweet cider or fruit juice may be used.

Baked Rice Pudding

Zapyechyennyi Risovyi Puding

175g (6oz) rice	Grated lemon rind
600ml (1 pint) milk	Good pinch salt
300ml (1/2 pint) water	Vanilla essence, to taste

Cook all the above ingredients in the top of a double boiler until the rice is soft.

40g (1 1/2oz) butter	Chopped almonds, to taste
3 egg yolks	Chopped candied peel, to taste
75g (3oz) sugar	3 stiffly beaten egg whites
1 tablespoon raisins	

Beat the egg yolks with the sugar and butter, then mix this into the rice. Add the raisins, peel and almonds. Leave to become cold. Fold in the egg whites. Turn this mixture into a crumbed loose-bottomed cake tin and bake at 190°C/375°F/Gas 5 for 40 minutes.

Serve with a sour fruit sauce, or with cherry jam.

The pudding is stiff enough to turn out like a cake.

RUSSIAN cooking

Pilau with Dried Fruit

Plov S Sushyenymi Fruktami I Mindalyem

225g (8oz) long-grain rice
Water
100g (4oz) dried apricots
25g (1oz) blanched almonds
75–100g (3–4oz) butter

25g (1oz) raisins
Few prunes
3 tablespoon clear honey
Salt

Wash the dried fruit and chop the almonds lengthways. Melt 25g (1oz) of butter, add the honey, the fruit and just sufficient water to cover the fruit. Cook gently for 20 minutes.

Bring the water to a fast boil, add salt and rice and cook until this is almost tender (about 10 minutes) keeping the water boiling fast all the time. Drain, return to the saucepan, add the remainder of the butter, stir the rice and butter together and put the pan into a warm oven (180°C/350°F/Gas 4). Leave until the rice dries out and finishes cooking. Serve on a hot dish, garnished with the stewed fruit.

The apricots used in this recipe are the small, dark round ones; but use what is available. There is no suggestion of soaking either the prunes or the apricots; soak the raisins for 5 minutes in hot water.

This type of sweet pilau may be used as a main course, or with meat, in particular lamb.

Pilau with Dill and Omelette

Plov S Ukropom I Omlyetom

225g (8oz) long-grain rice
900ml (1 1/2 pints) vegetable stock
50g (2oz) butter

Handful chopped fresh dill
2 eggs
Salt and pepper

Wash and coarsely chop the dill. Plunge it into boiling water and leave for 1 to 2 minutes. Drain. Cook the stock until boiling, then add the butter, dill and the rice. Cover and cook until the rice is tender and dry. Make a plain 2 egg dry omelette, roll this like a pancake, and cut into thin strips. At the last moment, when the rice is dry and soft, add the strips of omelette. Serve the rice on a hot platter.

To help the drying process of the rice, when it is soft, wrap the saucepan lid in a piece of absorbent cloth, then clamp it tightly on the pan and leave for at least 40 minutes on the side of the stove, or over the lowest possible heat.

Instead of adding the strips of omelette to the rice while it is in the pan, they can be added as a garnish when the rice is served.

Pilau with Capsicum and Tomatoes

Plov So Struchkovym Sladkim Pyertsyem

225g (8oz) long-grain rice
900ml (1 1/2 pints) vegetable stock
3–4 tablespoons vegetable oil
225g (8oz) mixed tomatoes
  and green peppers

1 large, finely chopped onion
Chopped fresh parsley, dill or other
  green herbs as garnish
Salt

Wash the rice in salted, boiling water, shake well and dry in a warm oven.

Heat the oil in a saucepan, add the onion and the rice, stir and fry until the rice begins to change colour with an almost transparent appearance. Take the pan from the stove, add the stock, return the pan to the heat, tightly cover and cook over a low heat until the rice has completely absorbed the liquid.

Peel and remove the seeds, etc., of the tomatoes and green peppers, and coarsely chop. Add these to the rice and continue simmering for at least another 40 minutes, or turn the rice into a casserole and finish off the drying process in a warm oven (180°C/350°F/Gas 4). Sprinkle with green herbs before serving.

RUSSIAN cooking

Pilau with Mushrooms

Plov S Gribami

225g (8oz) long-grain rice
900ml (1 1/2 pints) vegetable stock
100–150g (4–6oz) mushrooms

Butter or vegetable oil for frying
Salt and pepper

Clean and peel the mushrooms. Chop into fairly small pieces and lightly fry in butter, or oil, until half-cooked.

Bring the liquid to the boil, add the rice, the mushrooms and salt as required, cover tightly, lower the heat and simmer until all the liquid has been absorbed.

Sliced liver or kidneys may be added, or omit the mushrooms and use liver or kidneys instead, in which case this pilau ceases to be a mushroom one.

Pilau (Kazakhstan)

Plov Po-kazakhski

350g (12oz) lamb
225g (8oz) long-grain rice
750ml (1 1/4 pints) vegetable stock
100g (4oz) butter
1–2 chopped onions

100g (4oz) dried apricots or apples,
  unsoaked and chopped
225g (8oz) carrots, scraped and cut
  julienne style
Salt and pepper

Cut the meat into fairly small pieces. Melt the butter in a saucepan, add the onions and fry these until they begin to change colour. Add the salt and pepper, meat and carrots, and fry gently until the meat is half-cooked. Add the apricots, or apples, and finally the rice. Smooth down these ingredients, add the liquid, bring to the boil, stir, reduce the heat, cover and simmer for 40 minutes, or until the rice is quite tender and dry.

Just before serving, carefully mix the rice and the meat together again, using a large fork

Mutton Pilau, Yellow

Plov S Zharyenoy Baraninoy

225g (8oz) long-grain rice
900ml (1½ pints) water
175g (6oz) lamb (cut into
  small pieces)
75g (3oz) butter

1 large, chopped onion
Pinch saffron, soaked in water
Pinch cinnamon
Chopped fresh mixed green herbs
Salt and pepper

Bring the water, generously salted, to the boil, add the saffron and, when the water has turned yellow, add the rice. Bring once more to the boil, reduce the heat, cover the pan and simmer to let the rice absorb all the liquid.

Melt the butter, add the onion and fry until it changes colour, then add more meat, the herbs, cinnamon, salt and pepper. When the meat is brown, cover the pan and steam until the meat is tender.

Drain the rice, turn out on to a hot platter and serve, garnished with the meat and onion.

Pilau, Uzbek version

Plov Po-uzbyekski

450g (1lb) lamb
1–2 large, coarsely chopped
  onions
225g (8oz) long-grain rice,
  soaked for 2 hours

Cayenne pepper to taste
Salt
1 small grated carrot
900ml (1½ pints) water

Melt the butter and heat about one third of the onion. Brown this and put aside. Add the meat and brown; add the carrot and pepper, the rest of the onion, and sprinkle with salt. Cover and cook slowly, until the lamb is tender. Drain the rice, add to the pan, stir and, as the rice begins to change colour, add the water. Bring to the boil and cook uncovered. When no more liquid is left, wrap the lid in a cloth, clamp it tightly on the pan, draw the pan to the side of the stove and leave until the rice is quite dry. Turn out and garnish with fried onion.

RUSSIAN cooking

Noodles

Lapsha

450g (1lb) plain flour
3 egg yolks

Water
Salt to taste

Sift the flour into a bowl. Make a hollow in the centre, break in the egg yolks, add salt and mix these ingredients thoroughly. Gradually add enough water to make a firm dough. Leave this for 30 minutes. Turn the dough on to a floured board and roll out into a thin sheet. Leave this long enough to become dry, but not too long or it will crack. Sprinkle with flour, do this lightly, and roll the sheet of dough as you would a Swiss roll. Cut into strips, the width of these depends on future use. Open up the strips, shake off excess flour and leave until quite dry and firm. The noodles are now ready for use or for storing.

Noodles Boiled with Curd Cheese

Lapsha S Tvorogom

225g (8oz) noodles
75g (3oz) curd cheese

50g (2oz) salted butter
Salt and paprika pepper

Cook the noodles in boiling water until tender. Drain and return to the saucepan. Add the butter. When this has melted, add the cheese and gently stirring, cook until the noodles are again hot and completely covered with butter and cheese.

Serve sprinkled with paprika pepper.

Noodles Baked with Curd Cheese

Lapshyevnik S Tvorogom

225g (8oz) noodles
175g (6oz) curd cheese
1–2 eggs
1 tablespoon sugar

125ml (4fl oz) sour cream
Breadcrumbs
Butter for greasing
Pinch salt

Cook the noodles in boiling water until tender. Strain into a large bowl. While the noodles are cooking, sieve the cheese into a bowl, add the eggs, beat the mixture until smooth and creamy and add the sugar and salt. Pour this mixture over the noodles. Grease a baking dish and sprinkle it with breadcrumbs. Add the noodles with the cheese and egg sauce. Smear the top with some of the sour cream. Sprinkle generously with breadcrumbs and bake at 190°C/375°F/Gas 5 for about 30 minutes. Serve cut into slices and with sour cream.

To the cheese and egg mixture may be added vanilla flavouring, seedless raisins, or sultanas. To turn this dish into a savoury pie, omit the sugar and serve it with a tomato sauce mixed with sour cream.

Instead of breadcrumbs, biscuit or cake crumbs may be used.

Noodles with Honey

Lapsha S Myedom

225g (8oz) noodles
90ml (3fl oz) clear honey

75g (3oz) unsalted butter
50–75g (2–3oz) chopped walnuts
    or almonds

Cook the noodles in boiling salted water until tender, then strain. Return them to the saucepan, add the butter; when this has melted, add the chopped nuts. Separately cook the honey and pour this over the noodles. Bring gently to the boil, then pour at once into an earthenware dish.

RUSSIAN cooking

Siberian 'Ravioli' with Meat

Pyel'myeni

Pyel'-myeni are a speciality of Siberia and can be made hours, days or weeks in advance. Siberian housewives, I have been told, make them months in advance and store them in ice-cold cellars ready for anyone who may drop in for a meal.

275g (10oz) plain flour
2 egg yolks
6–8 tablespoons water

1/4 teaspoon salt
1/4 teaspoon pepper

Sift the flour, salt and pepper into a bowl, make a hollow in the centre and break in the egg yolks. Mix well, then gradually add the water to make a firm and very bland dough. Roll this out very thinly and cut into small rounds, each one should be roughly 5cm (2in) across. Leave in a cool place while you prepare the filling.

Filling

225g (8oz) each finely minced veal
  and pork

1 finely chopped onion
Salt and pepper to taste

Mix these ingredients together and moisten with a small amount of water. Put a little of the meat filling on to each of the rounds, fold over, press the edges together firmly and roll them up just slightly at the edges to prevent them opening. (In Siberia I am told that at this point the *pyel'myeni* are put outside to freeze, and freezing improves the flavour.) Drop into salted boiling water to cook and when the *pyel'myeni* rise to the surface they are ready, this takes 5 to 6 minutes. Remove from the water and serve at once with melted butter or sour cream.

Another sauce suggested for serving with the *pyel'myeni* is one of mustard thinned with a wine vinegar.

Although the recipe says the *pyel'myeni* take from 5 to 6 minutes to cook, it has been my experience that they take longer. Much depends on the quality of the flour used. Test before taking them all from the pan. What is meant by coming to the top of the water is that the *pyel'myeni* remain there while boiling.

Pyel'myeni are also offered with hot clear soups.

Stuffed 'Ravioli' (Ukraine)

Varyeniki

225g (8oz) plain flour
Milk or water
2 eggs

1 teaspoon sugar
Salt to taste

Sift the flour into a bowl, make a hollow in the centre and add 1 egg, salt and sugar, mix well, then add enough milk or water to make a firm dough, but not too stiff. Roll this out until it is about 6mm (1/4in) thick, and cut into long strips. Smear these with raw egg beaten with a little milk.

Filling

350g (12oz) curd cheese
1 tablespoon sugar

1 tablespoon sour cream

Beat these ingredients together and arrange the cheese along the lengths of the dough, leaving a little free to seal the edges. Fold over the edges to cover the cheese and with the fingers gently press around each mound. Cut between the mounds so that you have separate varyeniki. Turn out on to a floured board. Cook in salted boiling water for 5 to 6 minutes, remove and drain and put into a casserole. Dot with butter and serve in the casserole with sour cream.

Very like Italian ravioli, but served without grated cheese or tomato.

RUSSIAN cooking

Sour Cream and Curds
Molochnyye Blyuda

Sour Cream

Smyetana

The lavish use of sour cream in Russia, and other Slav countries, has made it an interesting feature of their cooking. It must be remembered that refrigeration is a comparatively recent innovation and cream spoils quickly. Instead of throwing away the spoiled cream, the Russians over the centuries utilized it in their cooking and they are so accustomed to its flavour that they prefer cream this way. It is used in almost every kind of dish, with meat and poultry, with vegetables and fish, with fruit and pancakes, with noodles. Just about everything can be improved, to the Russian culinary way of thinking, with sour cream. Many of their most delicious and delicately flavoured cakes and puddings owe their flavour entirely to sour cream.

In Britain today sour cream is readily available. But it can also be prepared at home. Simply leave as much cream as desired in a warm place and it will become sour. The time it takes to sour depends on the warmth of the room and the quality and freshness of the original cream. When the cream is sour it will keep in the refrigerator for up to a week. If you want to hurry the process of souring the cream, add a little lemon juice or sour milk to it.

Tinned cream can also be turned into sour cream. Warm the tin before opening, then pour the contents into a dish. Add a little strained lemon juice and keep in a warm place until the cream is sour.

Sour Milk

Prostokvasha

In Russia, as well as in other Slav countries, sour milk is considered a refreshing and nourishing drink. It is milk which has gone sour and there is nothing cranky about its use. It has much the same flavour as yoghurt and although the two are not identical, they are in certain circumstances interchangeable.

It is rare to find sour milk used to advantage, despite the fact that both in summer and winter milk often goes sour. Even in a refrigerator milk, if kept too long, will go sour. Often this milk is thrown away.

In English cooking there are several uses for sour milk, but it is seldom used as a drink, or as a sauce, or as a dressing, or as an aid to the roasting of meat and the cooking of vegetables.

Throughout the pages of this book there are recipes calling for sour cream. A substitute for this is thick sour milk instead, or curd cheese diluted with milk to a cream consistency.

In Russia milk is left in glasses and allowed to become sour and form a thick skin. Below the skin the milk is of a smooth, thick consistency. This is served chilled with grated cinnamon or nutmeg or both, together with slices of black bread.

Clotted Milk

Varyenyets

Pour at least 2.3 litres (4 pints) of fresh milk into a wide mouthed earthenware dish, or at least a nonmetallic dish. Place this in the oven at simmering temperature. Leave until a skin forms; push this down. Repeat this until the milk is thick and a soft brown colour. Cool, add sour cream to taste (this is purely optional) and put into individual glasses. Refrigerate and keep for 18 to 24 hours, or until it really thickens like Devonshire cream.

Serve sprinkled with rye breadcrumbs, or cakecrumbs and powdered cinnamon.

This is a country dish and popular with children.

As the milk evaporates, it is hardly worth while preparing clotted milk except with a large quantity.

RUSSIAN cooking

The Beautiful and the Good
(Raspberry-flavoured Sour Milk)

'La Belle et la Bonne'

1.2 litres (2 pints) thick sour
  milk or yoghurt
Raspberry syrup to taste

Handful washed and dried
  raisins
Handful grated coarse blackbread

Beat the milk with the raspberry syrup until it is foamy and the colour of the raspberry has almost disappeared. Add the raisins and the bread. Leave until very cold.

I was not able to discover the Russian name of this dish, which is meant for 2 people but could do for 3 or 4.

Whisked Sour Cream and Sugar

Smyetana Vzbitaya S Sakharom

150ml (1/4 pint) sour cream

2 1/2 tablespoons sugar, or to taste

Pour the cream into a basin and stand the basin in cold water or over ice. Beat steadily with the sugar until the cream thickens and doubles its bulk.

This cream may be flavoured with vanilla or may be whisked with enough fruit purée to give flavour and colour. Serve as a sweet dish, or as a sauce for puddings.

Sour Cream Pudding

Kryem Iz Smyetanye

600ml (1 pint) sour cream
175–225g (6–8oz) sugar

1 tablespoon gelatine
Vanilla flavouring to taste

Pour the sour cream into a basin, add the sugar and the vanilla flavouring. Place the basin on ice, or in very cold water. Beat the mixture until it is double its bulk. Dissolve the gelatine and gradually add this to the sour cream, beating continuously. Pour at once into individual glasses and leave to set. Serve with fruit compote, jam of any kind, or a fruit sauce. Instead of flavouring with vanilla a fruit syrup may be used.

Boiled Sour Cream Pudding

Puding So Smyetanoy (Varyennyi)

6 egg yolks	10 tablespoons sour cream
10 tablespoons sugar	175g (6oz) breadcrumbs
Grated lemon or orange rind	6 stiffly beaten egg whites
6 finely chopped, blanched bitter almonds	Butter for greasing pudding basin
3 tablespoons sultanas	Strawberry jam

Beat the egg yolks and the sugar together until thick and fluffy. Add the grated rind (to taste), the almonds, salt, sultanas, sour cream and finally the breadcrumbs. When this mixture has been well-blended, fold in the egg whites and pile into a greased pudding basin. Cook in boiling water for 1½ hours.

Turn the pudding out to serve and offer with it plenty of whole fruit strawberry jam.

I have experimented, with success, with plain yoghurt, also with sour milk when making this pudding, which is very light and not unlike our guards pudding.

The breadcrumbs should be fresh and preferably from brown bread.

Curd Cheese

Tvorog

For most of the following recipes, the curd cheese must be dry. If it is not sufficiently dry, wrap it in a piece of fine white cloth, put it between two plates with a weight on top and leave until every drain of liquid has disappeared.

Keep curd cheese as much as possible away from metal containers as it tends to take on the metallic flavour, although it is true this flavour

RUSSIAN cooking

disappears fairly quickly.

   Making curd cheese is a simple operation. Let a quantity of milk go sour (for example, 2.3 litres (4 pints) will yield up to 900g (2lb) of curd cheese). When it is thick and the curd well separated from the whey, hang it in a muslin cloth from the tap over the sink and leave it all night. By morning it will have dripped quite dry and be ready for use. To make it into cream cheese, mash into it some thick, fresh cream. If the weather is cold and the milk refuses to sour quickly, warm it and add a little lemon juice. Or you can add a little rennet. But the less rennet used, the more delicate will be the flavour of the cheese. A pinch of salt added just after the milk curdles will help the whey to separate.

   Nothing much seems to be done to the whey. In days gone by people considered a glass of whey good when feverish, and in the country, girls used it for washing their faces.

   Some people find that highly pasteurized milk, when sour, is very bitter. To this there is no answer.

Easter Dessert

Paskha

Paskha, the pride of Russian curd cheese cooking, is the traditional favourite Easter dish. It is not difficult to make and does not require any cooking.

450g (1lb) very dry curd cheese	150ml (1/4 pint) whipped cream
2 egg yolks	50g (2oz) butter
2.5cm (1in) piece vanilla pod	50g (2oz) blanched and chopped
100g (4oz) caster sugar	almonds
1 stiffly beaten egg white	

Slit the vanilla pod down the centre, take out the seeds and chop the beans.

   Cream the yolks until almost white with half the sugar. Add the chopped vanilla pod and seeds, cover and leave to stand. Cream the remaining sugar with the butter until pale and fluffy and the sugar completely dissolved. Beat into the egg yolks. Add the almonds, then gradually the cheese, taking care there are no lumps. When this is completely blended and the mixture smooth, add the cream and finally the egg white.

   Put all this into a perfectly clean piece of muslin cloth and pack into an equally clean flower pot. Wrap the muslin over the top of the curd mixture, put a weight on top and leave in a refrigerator for several hours, overnight is the best length of time. Excess whey will drip through the hole at the bottom of the flower pot. Turn out to serve and cut like an ordinary cake.

To this mixture some people add: raising, sultanas, glacé cherries, chopped candied peel, angelica, or slivers of almonds.

Traditionally the dessert, after being turned out, should be decorated with Easter symbols and with coloured hard-boiled eggs. In Russia there are special wooden moulds for this dessert, similar in shape to the flower pot (like a four sided pyramid), made of wood and embossed on the sides with Christian symbols, as, for example, the Orthodox Cross and the letters XB, Krhistos Voskryesye, 'Christ is Risen'.

Pistachio Dessert with Curd Cheese

Paskha S Fistashkami

700g (1½lb) dry curd cheese	100g (4oz) finely chopped
2–3 well-beaten eggs	pistachio nuts
100g (4oz) sugar	Vanilla essence
100g (4oz) butter	300ml (½ pint) double cream

Mix the cheese with sugar, add the eggs, cream, butter, vanilla and nuts. When thoroughly blended fill into a mould, or flower pot (like the Easter dessert) and leave in cold place until set.

Turn out to serve. If using a flower pot line it first with muslin.

If the cheese is lumpy rub it through a coarse sieve before using. The cheese may be served on its own or with whipped cream.

RUSSIAN cooking

Curd Cheese with Nuts (Salad)

Tvorozhnaya Massa S Oryekhami

450g (1lb) curd cheese
Toasted almonds
Little sugar

Pinch salt
Some finely chopped candied
  peel

Garnish

Chopped walnuts
Lettuce

Sliced, unpeeled oranges or
  tangerines

Sieve the cheese and mix with the almonds, sugar, salt and peel. Pile on lettuce leaves on plates. Sprinkle with chopped walnuts and surround with fresh, sliced orange or tangerine.

   For this recipe the cheese should not be too dry.

Curd Cheese Relish I

Tvorog S Syrom I

The following ingredients are mixed rather as taste dictates.

Curd cheese
Equal quantity any firm cheese

Sour cream
Salt

Rub the curd cheese through a sieve. Grate the firm cheese (almost any kind can be used with curd cheese). Mix the two types of cheese together, add salt and enough sour cream to blend the mixture. This relish can be served on its own or with a sour cream sauce.

Curd Cheese Relish II

Tvorog S Syrom II

Sieve curd cheese and mix with finely chopped or minced onion, and chopped green or red pepper. Add salt to taste. Spring onions are better in this recipe, especially if some of the fresh green stem, minced, is added. Serve as a spread with black bread.

Curd Cheese Relish III

Tvorog S Syrom III

Sieve curd cheese, add a little butter, salt and sour cream and caraway seeds.

Sweet Curd Cheese Fritters

Syrniki (Sladkiye)

450g (1lb) curd cheese
2 eggs
50g (2oz) castor sugar
Pinch salt and cinnamon

2 tablespoons plain flour
Butter for frying
Plain flour for coating the
   fritters

Garnish

Caster sugar and sour cream

Cream the eggs with the sugar until pale and fluffy. Rub the curd through a sieve into a bowl, add the 2 tablespoons of flour, salt and cinnamon and beat until the mixture is smooth. Melt about 75–100g (3–4oz) of butter. Take the curd from the bowl in tablespoons, drop into the flour, roll and slightly flatten on one side and shape into fritters. Fry at once, lightly brown on both sides, sprinkle with sugar and serve hot with sour cream, or a fruit sauce.
   Vanilla may be used instead of cinnamon.

RUSSIAN cooking

Sweet Curd Cheese Fritters

Tvorozhniki

450g (1lb) curd cheese
1 well-beaten egg
50g (2oz) caster sugar
Pinch salt

Plain flour
Vanilla to taste
50–75g (2–3oz) butter

Garnish

Caster sugar

Sour cream

Rub the cheese through a sieve into a deep earthenware bowl. Add to this 2 tablespoons of flour, the castor sugar, salt and the vanilla. Add the egg and mix well. Turn on to a floured board, roll into a thick 'sausage' and cut into 12 separate slices. Roll each slice very lightly in flour. Melt the butter and fry the slices on both sides until a golden brown. Serve very hot, sprinkled with castor sugar and with sour cream.

Instead of sugar and vanilla, caraway seeds are used when making savoury fritters.

Curd Cheese Potato Fritters

Syrniki Iz Tvoroga I Kartofyelya

175g (6oz) curd cheese
225g (8oz) cooked mashed
  potatoes
25g (1oz) plain flour
25–50g (1–2oz) softened butter

Salt and nutmeg to taste
Chopped fresh parsley and dill
1 beaten egg
Fine breadcrumbs
Butter for frying

Sieve the cheese and mix with the potato. Add the flour, the butter and knead to a smooth dough. Roll this into a salami shape, cut into slices, not too thick, dip in egg and coat with breadcrumbs. Fry in butter until golden brown on both sides.

Serve with spinach. If the slices are made smaller they make excellent cocktail snacks, especially for serving with beer or shandy.

Sweet Curd Cheese Tartlets

Vatrushki

This type of curd cheese tartlet can be made as a savoury, or sweet dish. When savoury, they are usually served as an accompaniment to borsh and other soups.

450g (1lb) curd cheese
2 egg yolks
25g (1oz) butter
1 tablespoon caster sugar

Grated rind 1/2 lemon or orange
25g (1oz) raisins
Pinch salt

Rub the curd cheese through a sieve, or beat it until smooth. Mix with remaining ingredients.

Pastry

450g (1lb) ready-made puff pastry

Roll out the pastry until it is quite thin and cut into squares, not too small, rather the size of our tartlets. Arrange the squares of pastry on a baking sheet and on to each piece of pastry drop a heaped teaspoon of the filling. Fold up the corners to meet the filling but not to cover it. Bake at 190°C/375°F/Gas 5 for 15 to 20 minutes. When the pastry is golden brown and leaves the baking sheet easily, it is ready.

Yeast pastry is rather more generally used than puff pastry in the preparation of Vatrushki, and instead of curd cheese, a jam or fruit filling may be used.

RUSSIAN cooking

Curd Cheese Pudding

Tvorozhnyi Puding S Oryekhami

450g (1lb) curd cheese
4 egg yolks
4 egg whites
3 tablespoons fine breadcrumbs
100g (4oz) caster sugar

50g (2oz) walnuts or almonds
50g (2oz) grated lemon or orange
  peel
75g (3oz) butter
1/2 teaspoon salt

Sieve the breadcrumbs, chop the nuts and lightly roast in the oven, or in a greased frying pan. Put through a grater. Mix with half the sugar. Clean the raisins, wash if necessary in warm water. Rub the cheese through a sieve and mix with the remaining sugar. Beat the butter and the egg yolks together until creamy and beat into the cheese. Add the breadcrumbs, grated rind, nuts and raisins. Beat the whites until stiff and fold into the cheese mixture.

Grease a basin with butter and sprinkle it with castor sugar. Pour the mixture into the dish, it should be three quarters full. Cover tightly and put the basin into a saucepan with enough water to reach approximately half way up the basin. Cover and cook over a fast heat for about 1 hour. The pudding is ready when it rises and begins to come away from the sides of the basin. Turn out on a hot plate and serve garnished with a fruit sauce.

A useful hint is to put some thick brown or parchment paper at the bottom of the saucepan. This prevents the pudding from burning.

Cheesecake

Vatrushka

350g (12oz) shortcrust pastry

Line a flan tin, or a cake tin (preferably with a loose bottom for easy turning out) and bake it 'blind' until half-cooked. Take from the oven and let it cool. Add the following filling.

450g (1lb) curd cheese	*2 stiffly beaten egg whites*
100g (4oz) caster sugar	*Vanilla to taste*
50g (2oz) butter	*Small quantity grated lemon*
2 beaten egg yolks	*or orange rind*

Cream the butter and sugar until fluffy, and the sugar has completely dissolved. Sieve the curd cheese and add this to the creamed butter. Add the egg yolks, the rind and the vanilla and, when the mixture is blended, fold in the egg whites. Pour this mixture into the half-baked pastry shell and bake at 190°C/375°F/Gas 5 until the top is a golden brown. Leave to cool in the oven, with the heat off and the door open. This prevents the centre from suddenly collapsing, which it often does.

The flavour can be varied by using blanched and chopped almonds, candied peel, sultanas or raisins.

Instead of pastry a biscuit base can be used.

RUSSIAN cooking

Pancakes
Bliny

Russian pancakes, or blinis, are for many of us our first introduction to Russian cooking. My own first meeting with them was in the best possible manner, spread with caviar and sour cream. For a long time I was under the impression that blinis were always served in this manner, and was most surprised to discover this is not usually the case.

One Russian broadcaster friend, struck by the suggestion of caviar-spread pancakes, confessed he had never eaten them, but agreed that such a manner of eating blinis must be very good indeed. However, one can and does still eat caviar-spread blinis in Russia, although it is more usual to spread them with other things.

The correct method of serving blinis is to stack them in a pile wrapped in a cloth to keep them warm, and offer with them a variety of items for individual spreading. Hard-boiled eggs, mashed sardines, salted or smoked salmon, sour cream, herrings, all can be spread over the warm, inviting blinis, served usually as part of the *zakuski*.

The usual size of the Russian pancake is about 15cm (6in) across and it is made in a small, thick-bottomed pan. Pancakes, although immensely popular with Russians of all classes, are considered to be indigestible. So, when indulging in a pancake eating session, one is advised to start with a bowl of clear soup and to eat the blinis to an accompaniment of several glasses of vodka.

It is important to eat blinis while they are hot; they toughen as they become cold.

Yeast Pancake

Bliny Na Oparye

225g (8oz) plain flour
300ml (1/2 pint) milk
1 tablespoon melted butter
1 egg yolk
1 stiffly beaten egg white

1/4 teaspoon salt
15g (1/2oz) yeast
150ml (1/4 pint) warm water
1 heaped teaspoon sugar

Dissolve the yeast in a little tepid water and mix in half the flour. Add the sugar. Cover and leave in a warm place to rise for about 1 hour.

When the yeast has risen, add salt, egg yolk, butter and the remaining flour. Knead the mixture until it is absolutely smooth. Gradually add the warm milk, stirring the mixture all the time. Cover and put again in a warm place to rise. When the batter has again risen, stir it and once more leave in a warm place. Do this three times, so that the dough rises and falls three times. Add the beaten egg white and leave for 15 minutes.

Grease a small frying pan very lightly with butter; when it is hot, pour into it a thin layer of the batter. As the pancake begins to fry sprinkle it with a little melted butter and turn it over to fry the other side. Serve very hot.

To make a 'drier' pancake, mix equal proportions of plain flour and buckwheat. The first dough is made with flour, adding 1 tablespoon of buckwheat only. After the dough has risen for the first time, continue as above.

'Baby' Pancakes

Blinchiki

225g (8oz) sifted plain flour
2 eggs
Pinch salt
1 teaspoon sugar

600ml (1 pint) milk, or half milk and
    half water
Butter for frying

Beat the egg yolks, salt and the sugar for 2 minutes. Gradually add the milk and stir this into the flour. Beat this mixture to a really runny batter, making sure there are no lumps. If there are, rub it through a sieve.

RUSSIAN cooking

Smear a small frying pan with butter and when it is hot drop about a tablespoon of the batter in the middle. Fry one side only to a golden brown. Turn the pancake out on to a floured paper or board, browned side up. Fold each pancake into flour or roll them, and return to the pan to be quickly fried again.

Very often the blinchikis are stuffed before being returned to the pan the second time. Choose any of the following fillings: curds mixed with egg yolk and raisins; minced meat flavoured with onion; stewed or puréed fruit.

Serve with sour cream, jam or a fruit sauce.

Drop Pancakes (Yeast)

Olad'i

15g (1/2oz) yeast
225g (8oz) plain flour
150ml (1/4 pint) warm milk
  or water

1 whole egg
1 tablespoon sugar
1/2 teaspoon salt
Butter

Dissolve the yeast in warm milk or water (preferably milk), add the flour and leave in a warm place to rise.

Beat the egg, salt, sugar and 25g (1oz) of butter together. Add to the yeast batter, but not until it has risen. Let it rise again. When the batter has risen for a second time, heat a little butter in the pan. Fry until a golden brown on both sides. The pancakes should swell and be very light.

To this basic mixture may be added raisins or chopped apple. *Olad'i* pancakes are small, rather like fritters.

Serve with sour cream, fruit purée or a fruit sauce, jam or honey.

Pancakes
Bliny

Quick-rising Pancakes

Bliny Skorospyelyye

225g (8oz) self-raising flour
450ml (3/4 pint) warm water
1 egg

1/4 teaspoon salt
1 teaspoon lemon juice dissolved
in 150ml (1/2 pint) water

Beat the egg in the water, add salt and sugar and stir this into the flour, beating all the time. Make quite certain there are no lumps in the mixture. Add the lemon-flavoured water and, when this has been absorbed, immediately start frying a little hot butter in a small frying pan. Use 1 good tablespoon of the batter for each pancake and fry on both sides until a golden brown.

Instead of water, sour milk may be used in the same proportion, but omit the lemon juice.

The original recipe called for plain flour with baking powder, but self-raising flour works just as well.

Cabbage Pancakes

Bliny S Kapustoy

Batter, make as for *blinchiki* (see page 169)

Filling

225g (8oz) firm white cabbage
1 finely chopped hard-boiled egg
25g (1oz) butter

Salt to taste
Milk

Wash the cabbage, discard the outer coarse leaves, cut into pieces, and remove the thick stalks. Finely shred the remaining cabbage. Sprinkle with salt and leave for 30 minutes. Squeeze dry. Melt the butter in a small saucepan, add the cabbage, simmer for a moment or so, then add just a small quantity of milk, enough to prevent burning. When the cabbage is tender and all the liquid has gone, it is ready for the pancakes. Take it from the heat, and into it mash the chopped hard-boiled egg. Keep hot.

Ladle 3 tablespoons of batter (to make 1 pancake) into a greased frying

RUSSIAN cooking

pan and fry on both sides to a golden brown. Put a generous portion of the cabbage on to each of the pancakes, fold over and simmer until the cabbage is reheated. Serve the pancakes with melted butter and sour cream.

The above quantity is meant for approximately 6 pancakes.

Pancake Pie

Blinchatyi Pirog

Pancakes in number and size as required, but generally 6 is sufficient. And any pancake recipe may be used.

Stuffing

Fry some finely chopped onion in butter or oil until soft. Add chopped celery, minced beef or lamb, salt and pepper. When this is thoroughly cooked, take from the heat and cool.

Make the pancakes. As they come from the pan, put them on to greaseproof paper and cover with a warm cloth. When all 6 pancakes are ready lay one at the bottom of a deep baking dish, spread with the meat and onion mixture, add another pancake and continue in this fashion until all the filling is used. The top layer should be a pancake. Put this into a moderate oven (190°C/375°F/Gas 5) for a short time (not too long or the pie will become dry) and just before serving pour over the pancakes some home made tomato sauce, which has to be generously mixed with sour cream.

The pancakes are best when at least 20cm (8in) across. Serve with peas and chip potatoes.

Pastry
Izdyeliya Iz Tyesta

Fundamentally there is not all that difference between pastry making in Russian cooking and in our own, except that the preference is for yeast pastry.

Although many of these Russian pastry dishes are not as often baked in Russian homes as they used to be, there are still ancient aunts and grandmothers who, when they can find the time and space in communal kitchens, make with loving care pastries and cakes; even, around Eastertime, the *kulitch*.

The following recipes, with one or two exceptions, are simple. Preparing yeast pastry is only a matter of practice and getting used to it.

Biscuit Pastry with Sour Cream

Biskvitnoye Tyesto Na Smyetanye

4 tablespoons caster sugar
2 tablespoons sour cream
1 egg yolk

1 tablespoon vegetable oil
10 tablespoons self-raising flour
1/2 teaspoon grated lemon rind

Beat the sugar and the sour cream, add the yolk and grated lemon rind. Beat well, sift the flour into a bowl, add the first mixture and mix well. A little more sour cream or flour may be needed to produce the right pastry consistency as flour, egg yolks and tablespoons vary considerably. Knead and keep the dough in a cold place for 2 hours before using.

This type of pastry, when baked, is crisp on the outside but spongy inside. Used mainly in making apple cake, cheesecake, etc.

Mille Feuilles, Russian style

Pirozhnoye Iz Sloyenogo Tyseta S Kryemom

450g (1lb) sifted plain flour
225g (8oz) unsalted butter
Pinch salt

1 egg yolk
125ml (4fl oz) lemon juice

Filling

225g (8oz) butter
175g (6oz) castor sugar
3 stiffly beaten egg whites, or
    equivalent in whipped cream

300ml (1/2 pint) thick custard
Chopped nuts, such as walnuts,
    almonds, etc
Toffee crumbs

Rub the butter into the flour, add the egg yolk, salt and lemon juice to make
a firm dough. Divide this into about 14 pieces, roll each piece into a ball
and then roll each ball into a round of paper thinness. Chill for about 30
minutes. 'Bake' each piece separately in a thick frying pan without any fat,
turning the pieces over in the same way as for a pancake. Do not let them
brown. Trim off untidy edges and crumble the trimmings. Keep for later use.

   Cream the butter and sugar, then add the whipped egg whites (or cream)
and custard. Take out 2 or 3 tablespoons of the filling and put this aside.
Smear 13 slices of pastry with filling and put one on top of the other until
they are all stacked. Cover with the remaining sheet of pastry, spread with
the rest of the filling, sprinkle with chopped nuts, toffee crumbs and the
crumbled bits of the trimmings.

Alexander Cake

Tort Alyeksandr

100g (4oz) butter
40g (11/2oz) sugar
Grated rind 1/2 lemon

275g (10oz) plain flour
Redcurrant jam or jelly
Sugar glaze

Beat the butter with the sugar until creamy and the sugar is dissolved. Add
the rind and the flour and mix to a firm dough. Roll this out and spread over

a baking sheet, slightly building up the edges. Bake at 230°C/450°F/Gas 8 until a light brown. With a serrated knife split into 2 layers. Spread one half of the pastry with the jam or jelly, cover with the remaining half and weigh down with a pastry board and leave for several hours. Before serving spread a sugar glaze over the cake.

Sugar Glaze

Dilute icing sugar with enough milk, cream or water to the consistency of a thin cream. Spread this with a pastry brush.

Alexander cake is an old-fashioned, much loved Russian children's cake. Instead of redcurrant jam or jelly, it can be filled with raspberry or apricot jam. Sometimes it was made in 3 layers, that is, 3 of pastry and 2 of jam. This recipe gives a short bread kind of pastry; other recipes suggest a yeast pastry.

Sweet 'Straws'

Khvorost

The Russian word *'khvorost'* means literally brushwood or twiglets, but in culinary terms it means straws. *Khvorost* brings back to me childhood memories, for they used to be the speciality of the Russian mother of a school friend, my first contact with Russian cooking. They should be crisp and flaky and are not for 'ladylike' eating.

225g (1lb) plain flour
50g (2oz) sugar
3 whole eggs
125ml (4fl oz) sour cream
  and milk mixed

Pinch salt
2–3 cooking apples
225g (1lb) lard for frying

Sift the flour in a heap on to a table or pastry board. Make a well in the centre. Add the eggs, sour cream and milk, sugar and salt. Mix well, then knead until the dough is smooth, the pastry is similar to that of noodles. Roll out the pastry until it is thin and cut into strips about 2.5cm (1in) wide and 7.5–10cm (3–4in) long. Twist each of the pieces in the centre, or make a slit in the centre of each piece and pull one end through the slit. Or make rings and twists in any fancied shapes.

Put the lard into a pan, add the apples, without peeling or coring, and bring the lard to the boil. Take out the apples; these are to be discarded. Drop into the boiling fat several twists of pastry and fry these until they are a golden brown. Drain on paper and sprinkle with icing sugar, or vanilla flavoured castor sugar.

Instead of using lard, vegetable oil may be used, and the apples omitted. Some more sophisticated recipes suggest less sour cream and milk, making up the liquid quantity with vodka. Vodka is much used in Russia in the making of cakes, especially chocolate cake, and also in pastry making.

'Wheel' Biscuits (Fritters)

Rulyet Biskvitnyi

25g (1oz) butter
25g (1oz) sugar
2 beaten egg yolks
Grated rind 1/2 lemon
1 tablespoon rum

1 teaspoon baking powder
75–100g (3–4oz) plain flour
Oil for frying
Caster sugar for dusting

Beat the butter and sugar together until creamy, add the eggs, rind, rum, baking powder and flour and mix to a firm dough. Knead until it comes away easily from the hands and the sides of the bowl. Roll out thinly, not too thinly, and cut into strips. Shape these into wheels or rings.

Heat the oil, drop in the 'wheels' and fry until a golden brown. Take from the pan, dry on absorbent paper, and toss in castor sugar. Serve immediately.

Warm the caster sugar before using.

Russian Pie I

Kulyebyaka I

The main difference between a Russian and a British pie is the shape and style of filling. The *Kulyebyaka* is higher and narrower, and the filling is in layers.

A typical Russian filling would be:

1 layer of boiled rice, or kasha
1 layer of meat, or fish

1 layer of sliced hard-boiled eggs

In order that the bottom of the pie should not become soggy, the first layer of filling should be dry, i.e. the rice; the next a juicy, or moist layer, such as meat, or fish; then the eggs, and again another of rice. All these ingredients are pre cooked.

The Dough

While generally a yeast or leavened dough is used, a flaky dough with a tendency towards being dry in texture (though not in richness) may be used. When rolled, it should be in a strip, the length of the baking sheet, of the usual pie thickness and about 15cm (6in) wide.

First prepare the pastry. The quantity is enough to serve 10 to 12 people, since a *kulyebyaka* is not an everyday pie and is usually meant for a number of people.

25g (1oz) yeast
1 teaspoon sugar

50g (2oz) plain flour
Tepid water

Mix the sugar with enough tepid water to dissolve the yeast. Make a hollow in the flour and pour in the yeast. Add 3 tablespoons more of the water and mix these ingredients together to make a dough. Shape this into a ball, cut across the top and leave covered in a bowl in a warm place to rise, until it doubles its size.

RUSSIAN cooking

Russian Pie II

Kulyebyaka II

175g (6oz) plain flour
3 lightly beaten egg yolks
Tepid water

100g (4oz) butter
1/4 teaspoon salt

Cream the butter. Sift the flour on to a board, make a well in the centre and drop in 2 egg yolks and about 2 to 3 tablespoons of tepid water. Mix these ingredients together and work to a dough, kneading all the while. Add the salt and the creamed butter and continue to knead the mixture until it is pliable. Combine this with the leavened dough and work the two together to a smooth mass. Put this into a bowl, cover with a cloth and leave in a warm place until it has risen again.

While the dough is rising prepare any of the fillings suggested at the end of this recipe.

Cut the dough into 2 equal portions. Roll into strips the same length as the baking sheet (roll hard, as yeast dough is rather rubbery and tends to spring back). Lay it on a lightly floured cloth, do this gently, then spread the stuffing along the centre of the pastry in layers. Brush the edges of the dough with beaten egg, bring the two sides together, pinch them tightly and, with the pastry still on the cloth, pick it up and turn upside down on to the baking sheet. The seam must be underneath and the joint well-pinched. Brush the top with beaten egg yolk and decorate with half-moons of pastry. Cover with a cloth and leave to rise again.

Or, take two thirds of the dough and roll this into a strip, arrange the filling in layers down the centre, roll out the remainder of the dough and cover the filling. Draw up the edges of the bottom layer of dough, moisten and pinch with the top layer. Make sure the stuffing is well-enclosed.

Just before baking, brush the top with egg yolk, pierce the dough in 3 or 4 places to let out the steam. Bake at 230°C/450°F/Gas 8 for 35 to 40 minutes. Take the *kulyebyaka* off the baking sheet, cover with a cloth and serve cold.

Fillings I

Nachinki I

With all of the following fillings use long-grain rice as well.

450g (1lb) uncooked minced beef or lamb	1–2 minced onions
50g (2oz) butter	Chopped fresh parsley
3 hard-boiled eggs	Salt and pepper

Melt the butter and lightly fry the onions, add the meat, put both through a mincer. Chop the eggs, add to the meat, add salt and pepper and chopped parsley.

Instead of minced beef, liver may be used, or poultry and other meats.

Fillings II

Nachinki II

1 small white cabbage	100g (4oz) butter
3–4 hard-boiled eggs	Salt and pepper

Clean the cabbage, remove the coarse outer leaves, cut into pieces, cut out the thick stalks. Shred remaining cabbage as finely as possible. Melt the butter, add the cabbage, and simmer until it is tender, stirring from time to time. The time it takes to become soft varies with the type of cabbage and the heat. The pan should be covered. Add salt and pepper just before serving. Coarsely chop the hard-boiled eggs and sprinkle these over the cabbage when filling the pie.

RUSSIAN cooking

Fillings III

Nachinki III

450g (1lb) salmon or other
  strongly flavoured fish
3–4 chopped hard-boiled eggs

50–75g (2–3oz) butter
600ml (1 pint) fish stock
Salt and pepper if required

Cook the fish in the stock until tender, take from the pan, and as soon as possible flake it, but make sure all bones are removed. Put the flaked fish into a bowl, add the butter, salt and pepper (if required) and finally the eggs.

Fillings IV

Nachinki IV

About 100–150g (4–6oz)
  spring onions
3–4 hard boiled eggs

Butter for frying
Salt and pepper

Chop the onions, using the green part as well, and fry in hot butter until they are soft but not brown. Add salt and pepper. Pile on to the pastry. Chop the eggs and sprinkle these over the top before enclosing the filling.

Fillings V

Nachinki V

900g–1.4kg (2–3lb) carrots
3–4 hard-boiled eggs
50–75g (2–3oz) butter

Salt and pepper
Chopped fresh parsley

Cook the carrots until soft in salt water. Drain and chop fairly coarsely. Melt the butter and lightly fry the pieces of carrot. Chop the eggs, mix altogether and spread over the pastry. Sprinkle with parsley, salt and pepper.
    All the above fillings are suitable also for an English type pie.

In a savoury *kulyebyaka*, *viziga* (*vizigo*) is generally used. This is the dried marrow of the sturgeon, and to most British palates, rather tasteless. Soak it in cold water until soft and pliable, about 2 to 3 hours. Strain, pour fresh water over it and cook for 30 minutes. While it is cooking it gives off an unpleasant smell of fish, but once it is cooled this smell disappears. Strain again.

Fry as many onions as required in hot oil, add the viziga and quickly fry this. Add pepper and chopped hard-boiled eggs, and spread this over whatever filling is being used.

Viziga is found in Britain under the name of Chinese vermicelli. It comes in long, very thin strands and is easy to cut. Russian friends of mine who have lived long in China have experimented with soy sauce with viziga and find that it adds both colour and flavour. They recommend it in the kulyebyaka, although it is not Russian.

Meat Tartlets, Kazakhstan Style

Belyashi

450g (1lb) plain flour
Just less than 300ml (1/2 pint)
  sour cream, water or milk
15g (1/2oz) yeast
350g (12oz) minced beef or lamb

2 minced onions
Pinch sugar
Salt and pepper
Oil for frying

Dissolve the yeast in a little warm milk, add the sugar and a little of the flour. Leave to rise until it doubles in size.

Prepare the stuffing:

Mix the beef and onions and add salt and pepper.

Sift the rest of the flour into a bowl, add the yeast batter and enough sour cream or other liquid to make a firm, pliable dough. Leave to rise again. Roll out the dough until quite thin and cut into rounds. Put a portion of the filling on each round, pinch up the edges to make small patties and leave to slightly rise again. Fry in very hot oil until brown on both sides.

RUSSIAN cooking

Fried Meat Patties

Chyeburyeki

These little patties are not exclusive by any means to the Russians. In Turkey they are an everyday dish, with all kinds of fillings and shapes. The Armenians also claim them as a national dish, and a similar type of fried patty is prepared and eaten in many parts of Asia, including India.

This particular recipe gives a minced lamb and onion filling, but any of the *kulyebyaka* fillings (see pages 177–8) may be used instead.

Filling

350g (12oz) lamb
Chopped fresh coriander
  or parsley
Water or lamb stock

Oil for deep frying
Salt and pepper
1 large onion
2 tablespoons cooked long-grain rice

Pastry

700g (1 1/2lb) plain flour
2 egg yolks
Salt

Water
1 beaten egg yolk

Keep the beaten egg yolk for brushing the top of the patties.

Put the onion, lamb and fat through the finest grinder of the mincer. Mix with the rice, salt, pepper and herbs. Add a little water, or stock to moisten.

Sift the flour into a bowl, add the eggs, a good pinch of salt and enough water to make a firm, pliable dough. Knead this, then roll out until it is paper-thin. Cut into rounds, the size depends on the individual, but generally these fried patties are small. Put a portion of the filling on one side only of each round of dough. Fold over and pinch the edges very firmly. Brush with beaten egg and fry in deep, very hot oil until brown.

Flat Cakes, Moldavian Style

Varyeniki Po-moldavski

Pastry

450g (1lb) plain flour
Water

3 tablespoons vegetable oil

Filling

225g (8oz) curd cheese
100g (4oz) butter
1 tablespoon plain flour
2 egg yolks

Salt to taste
Melted butter
Sour cream
150ml (1/4 pint) single cream

Rub the cheese and the butter together through a sieve. Beat the egg yolks, flour, salt and the milk together. Mix well, combine with the cheese and butter. Leave until required.

Sift 450g (1lb) of flour into a large basin (or on to a board), make a hollow in the centre, add the oil and, when this is combined with the flour, add enough water to make a stiff dough. Leave in a warm place for 10 minutes.

Roll out the pastry into a fairly thin square, or oblong. Sprinkle a napkin, or cloth with flour and lay the rolled out dough on it. Leave it to dry a little. Then cut into squares. On each square of pastry place a portion of the filling. Grease a baking sheet with butter, arrange the envelopes on this, brush each one with melted butter and bake at 190°C/375°F/Gas 5 until a light brown. Serve hot with cold, sour cream.

These flat cakes, or envelopes, are particularly popular in Moldavia. Fillings vary, some are made with goat's cheese, or with a mixture of cherries and cheese, or with stewed pumpkin.

Moldavian Meat Roll

Pirog Po-moldavski

450g (1lb) plain flour
3 well-beaten egg yolks

3 tablespoons cooled, melted butter
Tepid water

Sift the flour on to a board, make a hollow in the centre and stir in the egg, butter and enough water to make a firm dough. Knead until smooth. Sprinkle with flour, cover with a cloth and leave for 30 minutes.

Roll out the dough until it is a very thin sheet, then stretch it out carefully in all directions until the dough becomes as thin as cigarette paper. Place this on a cloth, sprinkle the pastry with melted butter and cover with the filling.

Roll up, like a Swiss roll or strudel, for this meat roll is very like an Austrian strudel, and place on a greased baking sheet and bake for about 30 minutes at 230°C/450°F/Gas 8 for about 30 minutes.

Filling

450g (1lb) minced, cooked beef or lamb
1–2 minced, fried onions

Salt and pepper

Combine these ingredients and moisten with a little tomato sauce, or cream (fresh or sour).

184

Little Pies or Patties I

Pirozhki I

These little pies are eaten on almost any occasion, and in the old days a positive mountain of them with varied fillings would be sent to the table. They are served hot or cold, offered with the soup, with the *zakuski*, with vodka and even at tea. In fact, scarcely a meal passes in Russia at which some variety of this kind of patty does not appear, or if not patties, one or other of the pies.

450g (1lb) plain flour	1 teaspoon sugar
About 300ml (1/2 pint) sour cream	1 beaten egg
50g (2oz) butter	1/2 teaspoon salt
2 eggs	

Sift the flour into a bowl or in a heap on to a pastry board. Cut in the butter and mix this into the flour until it disappears. Add the sour cream, sugar and salt, break in the 2 whole eggs and mix together to a firm dough. Roll this into a ball, cover with a cloth and put into a cold place for 30 minutes.

Roll out the dough to a sheet about 3mm (1/8 in) thick. Cut into small rounds and brush each round with beaten egg. Put a small portion of the stuffing in the centre or on the side of each round of pastry. Fold over and shape into a patty, they can be any shape, ovals, rounds or half-moons. Arrange these on a well-greased flat baking tin, brush the tops with beaten egg, and bake until a golden brown, 10 to 15 minutes.

RUSSIAN cooking

Little Pies or Patties II

Pirozhki II

450g (1lb) plain flour
450g (1lb) butter
6 tablespoons water

1/4 teaspoon salt
1 beaten egg

Mix these ingredients to a firm dough and leave in a cold place for 30 minutes. Roll out to 6mm (1/4in) thickness and cut into ovals or rounds, and continue as preceding recipe.

Fillings

Any of the fillings used in other patties, especially those for *kulyebyaka* (without the rice, naturally); or chopped hard-boiled eggs, chopped cooked fish, chicken meat, cabbage, all flavoured to taste. One country recipe is a mixture of finely chopped fried onion and very fat bacon, flavoured with salt, pepper, and crushed caraway or anise seeds.

Cakes and Biscuits
Izdyeliya Iz Tyesta

Easter Cake

Kulich

Although I have not made a *kulich* myself I have been an eyewitness at two or three *kulich*-baking sessions. On one occasion, watching my friend Maria, I was thrown out of the kitchen (with the rest of the family) for fear our presence might cause the temperamental *kulich* to fall flat.

The following description comes from this same Maria, who went through the *kulich* baking procedure step by step.

'Kulich,' said Maria, 'is made only once a year and you bake a whole lot in varying sizes, from the very large to the very small for presents. When making them, everything must be warm, and I mean everything.

'Among Russians we have terrific arguments as to which type of *kulich* is best. A light type of dry texture, a bit like the German sandcake, is one, and if you want this type of *kulich*, then you use a little saffron dissolved in vodka or other spirit. But the cake variety is generally more acceptable, at least I think so.

'And you must use butter. After all, *kulich* is made but once a year so it deserves the best in everything, ingredients as well as time, temper and temperament. And it requires real strength for kneading; you can't use an electric mixer because you make too much. So if you are not feeling too well, it is best not to tackle the *kulich*, you'll buckle at the knees and find your head swimming.

'Oh, and never use vanilla essence for the flavour, always the pods. Most people use almonds as well.'

With this preamble over Maria declared, 'The *kulich* must be made in stages.'

Stage I

75g (3oz) plain flour
1 tablespoon sugar

Boiling milk
1 egg yolk

RUSSIAN cooking

'Mix the flour and sugar together, add enough boiling milk to make a dough mass. Into this beat the yolk. Wrap up the bowl, cover it and put into a warm place, leave for 2 hours.'

Stage 2

150ml (1/4 pint) warm milk   1 tablespoon sugar
50–75g (2–3oz) fresh yeast

'Mix the sugar, milk and yeast, add this to the first dough. Mix it really well for this is the most important part of the proceeding. There must be absolutely no lumps. Put the bowl into a very warm place for 2 to 3 hours to allow it to rise.

'And there must be no draught. And no banging of doors, otherwise the shock causes the rising dough to flop. It requires mollycoddling. But it is not as difficult as it seems, at least to Russians, it is after all second nature to us, for *kulich* is made year after year.'

'Your culinary pride and glory?' I interrupted for the first time.

Maria nodded and continued her discourse. She did not like interruptions.

Stage 3

15 egg yolks   575g (1 1/4lb) unsalted butter
700g (1 1/2lb) sugar   10ml (3fl oz) olive oil

'All this must be mixed together so that it looks well-stirred, but it isn't. This must be added to the dough and you knead continually, adding between 1.8–2.3kg (4–5lb) of warmed plain flour and warmed milk.

'But with the milk you must use your own judgement; you keep the consistency always at dough level.'

Stage 4

1 whole dried vanilla pod   Glacé cherries (optional)
Raisins and sultanas   Candied peel (optional)
Almonds   5 egg whites

'Slit the vanilla pod lengthways and scrape out the inside. Coarsely chop the almonds. Clean and stone the fruit, chop the candied peel and the cherries. You've time to do all this while the dough is rising.

Cakes and Biscuits
Izdyeliya Iz Tyesta

'The amount of fruit and almonds should not be so much that you produce a regular fruit cake, or so little that you feel the cook stood on a hilltop and threw the fruit in, missing more than once.

'Add the fruit and almonds to the dough. Whisk the egg whites until stiff and then add these. And all the time knead and knead until the egg white has been incorporated.

'Cover the bowl with a clean cloth but do this loosely because the dough is going to rise and should not meet with any resistance. Now put the bowl into a nest of blankets and hot water bottles.' Maria laughed. 'First put a layer of blankets under the bowl, two at least, light but warm, and bring these half way up the side of the bowl. Between the blankets put the hot water bottles; again round the sides put more blankets to insulate the heat. Another blanket over the top (the lighter the blanket the better) and cover with an eiderdown. Leave to rise to almost 3 times its size, it will take time. When testing, make sure you exclude all draught; close doors, windows, etc.'

Stage 5

'Prepare the cylindrical tins. Grease these with butter, then line with greaseproof paper which has also been greased and sprinkled lightly with bread or cake crumbs. The paper should protrude at least 15cm (6in) above the top of the tins.'

Stage 6

'When the dough has risen turn it on to a floured tabletop, divide it into as many portions as you have tins, and knead each piece before putting it into the tins, which must not be more than a third full. It is better to grease too many tins than to overfill one, or to keep the temperamental dough waiting,' Maria declared.

Stage 7

'Put the filled tins in a warm place, cover with a cloth and, when risen to more than double the original size of the dough, put them into the oven.

'But the oven must be turned on at least 15 minutes before you want to use it,' she warned. 'The temperature should be 190°C/375°F/Gas 5. Small tins will take approximately an hour; the larger tins 2 hours.'

I asked, 'How do you manage to get all these *kulich* baked in an oven

189

without mishap?'

'First you put in the large tins. Then after 1 hour cautiously open the door. Whatever you do, you must not sneeze, or talk, or hardly breathe, and the door must be closed just as cautiously. It has happened that you are so pleased to see those blessed *kulich* rising that in sheer joy you slam the door. And down they fall. This is disaster. But this being such an annual ritual, you seldom take risks. Then, having the door open, you put in the small tins. In another hour both lots will be ready.'

'And then?' I asked

'You take them out and put the tins on to a wet cloth so that the cake doesn't stick to the paper and the paper to the tins. After about 5 minutes, take the tins off the cloth and put them on to a wire cake sieve and leave. If you try to get the cake out at this stage it might buckle.

'You test with a needle to make sure that the cakes are done, but remember, owing to the large quantity of butter the cake won't be absolutely dry, any more than a rich fruit cake is dry.

'You might find that the cakes brown too quickly, so put paper on the top of them. Turn the tins cautiously on their sides and roll the cakes out. Keep the greaseproof paper. Stand each cake on its base and put a clean, dry cloth over it. When it is completely cold (about 24 hours) you can return it to its original tin with the paper. Don't eat fresh *kulich*; it is kept for at least two weeks before eating.

'About a day or two before you actually want to use the *kulich*, you make an icing, the normal white of egg and icing sugar, and ice the cakes. There are two ways of doing this. Some families ice the cakes all over. Others, and we belong to this group, pour the icing on the top and let it drip down like candle grease. Then you complete the cake by adding the letters X-B, "Christ is Risen". The icing may be white or pink but preferably white.

'When you cut the cake, you cut it across, in rounds. First you cut off the icing top, and put this aside. Then you cut the slices for eating, and remember these slices are pretty big, so you will probably cut them in half again. Put back the icing top to keep the cake fresh.

'You start your *kulich* baking at about 7 o'clock in the morning and you must resign yourself to a day's constant care. You will have from this quantity of ingredients 2 large cakes, maybe 3 medium, and probably 2 small cakes. And this can be accomplished in an English kitchen with an average English cooking stove. I know, I have done it often.

'A *kulich* looks something like a chef's hat, or an orthodox priest's hat.'

Cakes and Biscuits
Izdyeliya Iz Tyesta

Russian Birthday Cake

Kryendyel' S Mindalyem

25g (1oz) yeast	1 teaspoon salt
900g (2lb) plain flour	100g (4oz) raisins
300ml (½ pint) warm milk	50g (2oz) ground sweet almonds
6 eggs	Vanilla pod, split and scraped
225g (8oz) sugar	Caster sugar
175g (6oz) softened butter	1 beaten egg yolk

Dissolve the yeast in the milk, add half the flour and leave in a warm place until it doubles in size. Cream the 6 eggs with the sugar and vanilla, add the butter and continue beating until this is thoroughly blended. Gradually beat in the remainder of the flour, add the salt, and finally combine this with the yeast dough. Knead the dough until it begins to come away from the basin, add the raisins, cover and again put in a warm place to rise.

When the dough has risen, turn out on to a board, sprinkle with flour, knead again and roll out. Shape with the hands into a plait and flatten the ends. Put on to a baking sheet and leave in a warm place for a few minutes. Smear with beaten egg yolk, sprinkle with almonds, put into a hot oven (230°C/450°F/Gas 8) and bake for 35 to 40 minutes. Before serving sprinkle with castor sugar.

Kryendyels are also shaped like the letter 'B', or curled round snake fashion.

Honey Cake

Kovrizhka Myedovaya

275g (10oz) self-raising flour	1 tablespoon ground walnuts or almonds
75g (3oz) brown sugar	Pinch cinnamon
175g (6oz) dark honey	Pinch ground cloves
2 eggs	1 tablespoon sour cream or milk

Beat the eggs until creamy, add the sugar and beat until thick. Add the honey, cinnamon and ground cloves and beat all this until smooth. Add the flour and beat for a full 5 minutes.

191

Pour this mixture into a square or rectangular greased cake tin, sprinkle the top with ground nuts and bake at 230°C/450°F/Gas 8 for 20 to 30 minutes.

Serve cold, sliced like bread. Sometimes the Russians smear slices with plum jam (see page 217), put the slices together again and cover the cake with a royal or sour cream icing.

Although technically a cake, this recipe produces a firm texture, more like bread, and extremely good. The nuts should be coarsely ground.

Rum Baba

Baba Romovaya

25g (1oz) yeast	Sugar
Warm milk	225g (8oz) sifted plain flour

Dissolve the yeast with a little sugar and warm milk, add half the flour and mix until smooth. Cover with a cloth and leave in a warm place until the batter rises.

50g (2oz) sugar	2 stiffly beaten egg whites
2 beaten egg yolks	Pinch salt
75g (3oz) butter	

Cream the butter with the sugar, add the egg yolks, the rest of the flour and the yeast dough. Fold the egg whites into the dough and knead it until it is smooth and firm. Cover and leave again in a warm place to rise. Put it into a well-greased, small but tall baking tin. Leave again for 15 minutes. Bake at 220°C/425°F/Gas 7 for about 30 minutes, or until the baba is a golden brown.

Syrup

225g (8oz) sugar	150ml (1/4 pint) rum
150ml (1/4 pint) water	

While it is cooking prepare a syrup. Put the sugar, water and rum into a pan and bring to the boil. Cook until the syrup is thick.

Turn the baba out of the tin and, while it is still hot, pour over it the hot syrup. When the syrup has thoroughly soaked into the baba, sprinkle it generously with powdered sugar.

Serve hot or cold.

A few seedless raisins and vanilla flavouring may be added.

Walnut Cake

Tort Oryekhovyi

450g (1lb) shelled walnuts
9 eggs
225g (8oz) icing sugar

2–3 tablespoons plain flour
1 tablespoon rum

Grind the nuts. Separate the yolks of the eggs from the whites. Beat the yolks with the sugar until stiff and almost white. Add the nuts and the flour and blend thoroughly. Beat the whites until stiff, then fold these into the walnut mixture. Line a large cake tin with greased, greaseproof paper, pour in the mixture and bake at 190°C/375°F/Gas 5 for 1 hour.

Turn the cake out of the tin, leave until cool. Slice off the top and cover the base with the following filling. Return the top.

Filling

300ml (1/2 pint) single cream
Vanilla to flavour
175g (6oz) sugar
3 egg yolks

About 20 almonds blanched
  and finely chopped
50–75g (2–3oz) walnuts blanched
  and finely chopped

Put the cream in the top of a double boiler, add the sugar, and vanilla, and cook over hot water until only half of the cream remains. In the meantime beat the egg yolks and stir these into the cream. Add the almonds and walnuts. Mix well, but do not allow to boil or the egg yolks might curdle.

Some of the walnuts can be left whole and the top of the cake decorated with these. When adding the egg yolks it is always a good plan to take the pan from the stove to avoid calamity.

Walnut cake is rich and light and can be served as a sweet at luncheon or dinner.

RUSSIAN cooking

Biscuits

Pryaniki

3 eggs
175g (6oz) plain flour

Cardamom or vanilla to taste
Grated lemon rind

Cream the eggs and sugar until almost white. Add the flavouring and the flour and mix well. Take teaspoons of the mixture and drop them on to a greased baking sheet, with spaces of 2.5cm (1in) between each. Bake at 230°C/450°F/Gas 8 for 7 to 10 minutes. Remove from the baking sheet with the tip of a knife.

These little biscuits are usually smeared with a light icing, and sometimes flavoured with peppermint. They are exceedingly popular among Russians. In shape they are like large buttons. At village fairs they used to be made in the shape of various barnyard animals, chickens, etc.

The texture is rather sticky and spongy.

Sauces
Sousy

There is a good variety of sauces in Russian cooking, perhaps the result of the once strong French influence in Russia.

There was a time when all the best cooks were French and the Russian aristocracy spoke French as well as ate French. But although the French influence is there, there is really not much which is absolutely French about most of these sauces, which are satisfying, interesting but seldom subtle.

I think in some ways the Russian sauce is akin to the Indian curry, it is an endeavour to make bland food taste good and, in my opinion, a thoroughly satisfactory effort.

White Sauce (Basic)

Byelyi Sous

25g (1oz) butter
25g (1oz) plain flour
600ml (1 pint) fish stock

1 tablespoon single cream
1 tablespoon lemon juice

Melt the butter, add the flour and stir until blended. Gradually pour in the stock, stirring all the time to a thick sauce. Take the pan from the heat, add the cream and, finally, the lemon Juice.

When using fish stock the lemon juice is essential. Instead of cream, a knob of butter can be used. Grated nutmeg and pepper is often added.

More or less lemon juice may be used, it is according to taste.

RUSSIAN cooking

Tomato Sauce I

Tomatnyi Sous I

600ml (1pint) hot, white sauce
  (see page 195)
25g (1oz) butter
300ml (½ pint) tomato juice
1 chopped onion
1 chopped carrot

1 chopped piece parsnip
1 teaspoon sugar
1 teaspoon lemon juice
1 bay leaf
Cayenne pepper to taste
Salt

Melt the butter, simmer the chopped vegetables until soft; add the tomato juice and continue cooking slowly for 20 minutes, stirring from time to time. Add salt, sugar, lemon juice, bay leaf and pepper. Strain. Mix with the white sauce.

Tomato Sauce II

Tomatnyi Sous II

Tomato sauce, prepared as above
50g (2oz) sliced mushrooms
1 pickled diced cucumber

Stoned green, chopped olives
  to taste
1 teaspoon mashed capers

Pour boiling water over the cucumber, bring to the boil and strain. Mix with the above ingredients and simmer for about 10 minutes.

Serve with fish.

About 150ml (¼ pint) of Madeira may be added if desired, just before serving.

Checking carefully through the tomato sauce recipes I found that nearly all were mixed with a fish stock. However, meat stock can be used when the sauce is required for a meat or vegetable dish where the flavour of the fish would be objectionable.

Tomato Sauce for Meat

Tomatnyi Sous III

450ml (3/4 pint) tomato juice
25g (1oz) butter
1 small carrot
1 small parsnip diced
1 small onion

1 teaspoon tomato ketchup
25g (1oz) plain flour
300ml (1/2 pint) beef or lamb stock
Salt and pepper

Melt the butter, add the vegetables and simmer until they begin to change colour; sprinkle with flour and gradually add the tomato juice. Mix well, add the stock, stir and cook slowly for 10 minutes. Just before it is ready, add the salt, pepper and ketchup and a small knob of butter. Strain.

Red Sauce (Basic)

Krasnyi Sous Osnovnoy

600ml (1 pint) brown meat stock
4 tablespoons tomato purée
50g (2oz) butter
1 minced carrot
1 minced onion

1 tablespoon plain flour
1 teaspoon sugar
Salt and pepper
Small piece parsnip

The stock, it is advised, should be made from the left-over bones of roasted or fried meat. Take from it 150ml (1/4 pint), leave until cold and stir into the tomato purée. The rest of the stock should be hot and, of course, strained. Put the sugar into a small pan over a good heat and slightly burn it.

Melt the butter, add the onion, cook until it begins to change colour, add the flour and stir until blended. Gradually add the hot stock, stirring all the time. Bring to the boil. Add the burnt sugar, the tomato purée (diluted with cold stock), salt and pepper and cook for 15 minutes over a moderate heat. Strain and return to the pan to reheat.

This sauce, which is excellent with steaks, rissoles, etc, is mainly used as a basis for other sauces, in particular Madeira wine sauce.

RUSSIAN cooking

Basic Mushroom Sauce

Gribnoy Sous

25g (1oz) dried mushrooms
600ml (1 pint) white sauce
  (see page 195)

Salt and pepper
1 small, minced onion lightly
  fried in butter

Wash the mushrooms in hot water and soak in a little water or milk overnight. Next morning drain, slice them finely and cook until soft (keep the liquid) Bring the white stock to the boil, add the sliced mushrooms, the liquid and the stock, salt and pepper, and onion.

Used with potato dishes. The onion may be omitted.

To this basic sauce may be added:

75g (3oz) stoned prunes
25g (1oz) seedless raisins
1 teaspoon sugar

100g (4oz) tomato purée
1 teaspoon vinegar (optional)

Cook the above ingredients in a little water until the fruit is soft, rub through a sieve and add to the basic mushroom sauce.

Or, more simple, is mushroom sauce with tomato and onion:

Basic mushroom sauce
Tomato purée to taste
1 bay leaf

6 peppercorns
1 large, chopped onion
Butter

Melt enough butter to fry the onion until it is soft but not brown. Add the tomato purée, the peppercorns and the bay leaf and finally stir in the basic mushroom sauce. Cook until the onion is soft. Serve as it is, or rubbed through a sieve.

Salted Cucumber Sauce

Rassol Sous

50g (2oz) butter
25g (1oz) plain flour
1 teaspoon finely chopped
  fresh parsley
300ml (1/2 pint) vegetable stock

150ml (1/4 pint) strained
  cucumber brine
50ml (2fl oz) dry white wine
2 diced pickled cucumbers
Salt and pepper to taste

Melt the butter, add the flour and, when this is blended, add the parsley and gradually pour in the strained stock.

Stirring all the time, cook this over a gentle heat for 5 minutes. Add the brine, wine and finally the cucumbers. Bring to the boil, add salt and pepper, stir once more, and serve hot.

Serve with roast beef, pork, or duck.

The wine should not be sweet, but should tend towards being sweet.

Egg and Butter Sauce

Yaichno-maslyanyi Sous

75g (3oz) butter
2–3 well-beaten egg yolks
1 tablespoon lemon juice

Cold water
Salt and pepper

Put 90ml (3fl oz) of cold water into the top of a double boiler. Stir the egg yolks into this. When completely mixed, add the butter, salt and pepper and bring to the boil, stirring all the time with a wooden spoon. As the sauce begins to thicken, remove it from the heat, add the lemon juice, stirring vigorously all the time.

Used with cauliflower and asparagus, poultry and fish, and with leeks cooked as asparagus.

RUSSIAN cooking

Egg and Wine Sauce

Yaichnyi S Vinom Sous

3 egg yolks
200ml (3fl oz) dry white wine
1 teaspoon strained lemon juice

50g (2oz) caster sugar
Thin strip lemon rind
Pinch salt

Beat the yolks, add the sugar and beat the mixture until thick. Add the rind and gradually the wine, beating all the time. Put this mixture into the top of a double boiler, add salt and cook over hot, but not boiling, water until the mixture thickens, stirring constantly. Take the pan from the heat, add the lemon juice and return the pan to the heat for a minute or so longer.

Serve with fish, or chicken.

To make a more foamy sauce, beat 3 egg whites until stiff, fold into the sauce after the lemon juice and cook for 2 to 3 minutes.

This sauce can also be served with stewed fruit, especially a rather sour apple compote, and fruit kissers.

Horseradish Sauce with Beetroot

Khryen Sous So Svyekloy

100g (4oz) horseradish
75g (3oz) grated, cooked beetroot
50ml (2fl oz) vinegar

300ml (1/2 pint) boiling vegetable stock
Salt and sugar to taste
1 teaspoon English mustard powder

Wash and brush the horseradish and soak for 1 hour in cold water. Scrape it finely with a sharp knife (this process brings tears, as when peeling onions) Put the grated horseradish into a deep dish and pour the stock over it; cover with a tight fitting lid. Leave until it cools. Add vinegar, mustard, salt and sugar and stir. Finally add the beetroot.

Use with roast pork, cold meat such as beef, cold fish and all aspic dishes.

Horseradish and Sour Cream Sauce

Khryen Sous So Smyetanoy

2 tablespoons grated horseradish
25g (1oz) butter
25g (1oz) plain flour
300ml (1/2 pint) sour cream

1 teaspoon lemon juice
300ml (1/2 pint) vegetable stock
Salt and pepper

Wash and grate the horseradish and soak in cold water.

Melt the butter, add the flour, blend and gradually add the stock. Bring this to the boil, stirring all the time; take the pan from the heat and add the grated horseradish. When this is thoroughly blended, add the sour cream. Return to the heat, stir in salt and pepper and bring the mixture almost to the boil. Remove the pan from the heat before adding the lemon juice.

Serve with tongue, or other boiled meats.

Lemon Sauce

Limonnyi Sous

25g (1oz) butter
1 small, finely chopped onion
25g (1oz) plain flour

600ml (1 pint) vegetable stock
Thinly cut rind 1/2 lemon
Juice 1/2 lemon

Melt the butter, fry the onion and, as it begins to soften, sprinkle in the flour. Stir this until the mixture is blended; then gradually add the bouillon and the lemon rind. Bring to a slow boil. Rub through a sieve, stir in the lemon juice, reheat and serve hot.

Serve with fish.

RUSSIAN cooking

Onion Sauce with Sour Cream

Smyetannyi Sous S Lukom

1–2 minced onions
150ml (1/4 pint) sour cream
25g (1oz) butter
25g (1oz) plain flour

1 teaspoon wine vinegar
Vegetable stock
1/2 teaspoon salt
1/2 teaspoon English mustard

Melt the butter, add the flour but do not let either change colour as this sauce should be as white, or creamy coloured as possible. Gradually add the stock and onions and simmer. Add the sour cream, salt, mustard and vinegar, bring to the boil and again simmer for 10 minutes.

Serve with lamb, rissoles, boiled cabbage, potatoes or cauliflower.

Sour Cream Sauce I

Smyetannyi Sous I

600ml (1 pint) sour cream
25g (1oz) butter
25g (1oz) plain flour

1 small, minced onion
Salt and paprika pepper
150ml (1/4 pint) dry white wine

Melt the butter, add the onion and cook gently until the onion begins to soften. Sprinkle with flour. Add the wine and continue cooking slowly until the onion is soft. Stir in the sour cream and when this is completely blended into the sauce, add salt and paprika pepper. Strain before serving.

Serve with plain boiled cabbage, cooked veal, lamb and tongue, and with stuffed cabbage leaves (see pages 88–9)

Sour Cream Sauce II

Smyetannyi Sous II

600ml (1 pint) sour cream
25g (1oz) butter

25g (1oz) plain flour
Salt and pepper

Melt the butter in the top of a double boiler, add the flour; when blended, gradually add the sour cream. Bring slowly to the boil, add salt and pepper and cook until the mixture is thick. To this sauce tomato purée can be added.

Serve with almost anything, fish, liver, rissoles and cutlets, also with steaks and roast game.

Sour Cream Sauce III

Smyetannyi Sous III

300ml (1/2 pint) sour cream
25g (1oz) butter
Salt

300ml (1/2 pint) vegetable stock
25g (1oz) plain flour

Melt 25g (1oz) of butter in the top of a double saucepan, add the flour and, when this is blended, stir in the stock. Bring this to the boil, gradually add the sour cream and simmer for 10 minutes. Just before serving, add salt and remaining butter.

A small quantity of tomato purée may be added.

RUSSIAN cooking

Sour Cream Sauce with Onion and Tomato

Smyetannyi Sous S Tomatom I Lukom

300ml (1/2 pint) sour cream
1 large, finely chopped onion
25g (1oz) butter

2 tablespoons tomato purée
Salt and pepper

Melt the butter, add the onion and simmer until partially cooked. Add the tomato purée, salt and pepper to taste. Cook gently for 5 to 7 minutes. Add the sour cream and simmer for another 10 minutes.

This sauce is used mainly with golubsty but goes with other vegetables, especially boiled cabbage.

Sweet and Sour Sauce

Kislosladkii Sous S Oryekhami

100g (4 oz) prunes
300ml (1/2 pint) strained stock
1 level tablespoon brown sugar
Juice 1 lemon or 2 tablespoons
  vinegar

50g (2oz) raisins
50–75g (2–3oz) chopped walnuts
Salt and pepper to taste

Soak the prunes in a little water overnight. Strain (keep the water) and remove the stones. Cook until soft in the liquid in which they were soaking and rub through a sieve.

Return the sieved prunes to the pot, add the stock and remaining ingredients, bring the mixture to the boil, lower the heat and simmer for 10 minutes.

Serve with boiled ham, game, cold meats and fish.

Grated horseradish (to taste) is sometimes added.

Vinaigrette Sauce

Vinyegryet Sous

1 hard-boiled egg
2 tablespoons olive oil
2–3 tablespoons vinegar
1/2 tablespoon capers
2 tablespoons diced fresh
   cucumber

1 teaspoon finely chopped onion
1/2 tablespoon chopped fresh tarragon
   or parsley
1/2 teaspoon sugar
Salt and pepper

Separate the yolk from the white, and finely chop the latter.

Sieve the yolk (or mash it until smooth), add salt and pepper and enough oil to mix to a paste. Dilute this with vinegar, add the egg white, capers, onion, parsley (or tarragon) and the cucumber.

Serve with cold fish, cold cooked pork, and hot roasts, or boiled pork and veal.

Almond Sauce

Mindal'nyi Sous

600ml (1 pint) milk
75g (3oz) sweet almonds
Few bitter almonds

2 egg yolks
50–75g (2–3oz) sugar, or to taste

Put all the almonds into a pan and cover with boiling water. Leave for 15 minutes, strain and blanch. Drop into cold water and leave for 2 to 3 hours. Put through a grinder.

Put the ground almonds into a saucepan. Gradually add the milk. When the milk and almonds are blended and the milk has come once to the boil, take the pan from the heat. Leave until the milk has cooled, then strain the mixture through a muslin cloth. (The almonds can be used later in stuffing apples.)

Cream the yolks with the sugar until the mixture is almost white. Bring the almond-flavoured milk to the boil then stir it into the eggs. Return the mixture to the pan. Stir with a wooden spoon and cook gently until the sauce reaches almost boiling point.

Almond sauce can be used hot or cold, with puddings and other sweet dishes.

RUSSIAN cooking

Fruit Sauce

Fruktovyye Sousy

This is one of the simplest of the Russian sauces. Apples, peaches, pears or plums, quinces, etc are peeled and cored and stewed gently in a minimum of liquid until soft. They are then rubbed through a sieve, sugar added, the purée again gently brought to the boil, and the sauce served hot or cold. Strained lemon juice, red wine, or vodka is often added.

This type of sauce is usually eaten with sweet dishes, puddings, etc, but occasionally mayonnaise is added and the sauce is used in conjunction with salads.

Dried Apricot Sauce

Sous Iz Kuragi

225g (8oz) dried apricots	75–100g (3–4oz) sugar, or to taste
600ml (1 pint) water	

Wash the apricots, put them into a saucepan, add the water and leave overnight, or until the apricots are swollen to their original size. Cook the fruit until soft over a moderate heat. Rub through a sieve, return to the pan, add sugar and cook over a low heat, stirring all the while, until the sugar has completely dissolved.

This sauce may be used either hot or cold, and with most kinds of puddings.

Blackcurrant Sauce

Chyernosmorodinovyi Sous

600ml (1 pint) basic red sauce
150ml (1/4 pint) red wine
150ml (1/4 pint) vegetable stock
Butter
50g (2oz) blackcurrant jam
225g (8oz) ham bones

Sprig each fresh parsley
  and tarragon
6 peppercorns
1–2 bay leaves
Salt if required

Crush the bones and lightly fry in a little butter. Add the wine and the stock, the peppercorns, bay leaves, parsley, tarragon and the jam. Bring to the boil and simmer for 20 minutes. Add the red sauce, salt (only if required) and bring to the boil. Cook for 5 minutes, strain and add a small knob of butter.

Serve hot with game, hare, rabbit, etc.

Cherry Sauce (Baltic-Russian)

Vishnyevyi Sous

225g (8oz) stoned cherries
300ml (1/2 pint) water
150ml (1/4 pint) Madeira

1 teaspoon grated lemon rind
1–2 teaspoons cornflour
75–100g (3–4oz) sugar

Crush 3 to 4 of the cherry stones and add the kernels to the cherries. Put into a pan and cook in the water until very soft. Rub through a sieve and return to the pan. Add the wine, lemon rind and sugar. Mix the cornflour with enough water to make a thin paste. Stir this into the cherry purée and bring it slowly to the boil. Cook over a medium heat until the sauce is thick.

Served with steamed puddings, rum babas or pancakes.

This sauce may easily be prepared with tinned or bottled cherries. Use the liquid in which they are preserved, and sugar as required. Some recipes also add sour cream, which gives a slightly different, but pleasant flavour.

RUSSIAN cooking

Fresh Berry Sauce

Sous Iz Svyezhikh Yagod

225g (8oz) fresh berries
  (strawberries or raspberries)
600ml (1 pint) water

100g (4oz) sugar, or to taste
2 teaspoons cornflour

Clean the berries and rub them through a sieve. Bring the sugar with the water to the boil and add the sieved fruit. Mix enough water with the cornflour to make a thin paste. Stir this into the simmering fruit, continue stirring, bring gently to the boil, let the sauce thicken, then take from the heat.

Serve hot or cold. Recommended with buckwheat, rice dishes and pancakes.

Blackcurrant and Apple Sauce

Fruktovo-yagodnyi Sous

100g (4oz) blackcurrant jam
125ml (4fl oz) apple sauce
  or purée
50g (2oz) diced onion
1 teaspoon wine vinegar
2 whole oranges
1 lemon

150ml (1/4 pint) port or other
  red wine
1/2 teaspoon English mustard
Pinch pepper
Powdered ginger to taste
Ground cloves to taste

Rub the jam through a sieve. Cook the onion in a little water and the vinegar until soft. Grate the peel of the oranges and the lemon and pour boiling water over the rind. Cool. Drain off the liquid and add the port. Leave for 1 hour.

Squeeze the oranges and lemon. Strain the juice.

Mix the jam, apple sauce, onion, fruit juice, pepper, mustard, ginger, cloves and the grated rind.

Serve cold with cold meats, especially game and pork.

Instead of jam, concentrated blackcurrant may be used in the equivalent quantity.

The above quantity makes quite a lot of sauce. It keeps well in a refrigerator, and goes well with lamb.

Walnut Sauce I (Georgian)

Oryekhovyi Sous (Satsivi) I

225g (8oz) coarsely chopped
  walnuts
175g (6oz) minced onions
3 well-beaten egg yolks
Chopped garlic to taste
600ml (1 pint) strained
  chicken stock

Pinch cinnamon and
  powdered cloves
1 bay leaf
Cayenne pepper to taste
50g (2oz) butter
25g (1oz) plain flour
1 tablespoon wine vinegar

Melt the butter, add the onions and cook over a low heat until soft but not
brown. Add the flour and stir this until blended with the butter and onions.
Add the stock, do this gradually, stirring all the time, and continue to cook
gently for 10 minutes. Add the vinegar, garlic, cinnamon, cloves and pepper,
and the walnuts. Stir well and simmer for 5 minutes. Take the pan from the
heat and stir in the egg yolks. Bring the sauce slowly once more to the boil.

Serve hot with poultry, especially chicken, or turkey, vegetables, or meat.

Finely chopped fresh parsley is often added to this sauce, and spring
onions are usually preferred to the ordinary onion.

Salt is not added, unless the stock is not sufficiently salted.

Walnut Sauce II (Georgian)

Oryekhovyi Sous (Satsivi) II

450g (1lb) shelled walnuts
600ml (1 pint) chicken stock
Salt and cayenne pepper

1–2 slices white bread soaked
  in chicken stock

Coarsely grind the walnuts. Squeeze the bread until dry. Put these ingredients
together through a mincer. Add enough chicken stock to make a thick sauce
(but a sauce which will pour) and salt and pepper to taste.

This type of sauce is poured over strips of cold chicken and the above quantity
is enough to cover 1 large chicken or small turkey or 2 small chickens. Serve cold.

Serve as a main course, but without any accompaniment.

RUSSIAN cooking

Wild Plum Sauce

Tkyemali Sous

225g (8oz) plums
1 crushed clove garlic

Salt and pepper
Chopped fresh basil and coriander

Wash the plums and simmer in a little water until soft. Rub through a sieve, return to the pan, add salt, pepper, garlic, basil and coriander, and enough of the liquid in which the plums were cooked to make a sauce. Allow to cool before using.

This is a sharp and sweet sauce used mainly with boiled meats, *shashlik* and other grills.

Wild plums grow in the Caucasus and are much used for making sauces. They can be bought fresh and tinned. Failing these wild plums, you can use prunes, fresh or dried, or really sour damsons. Sour cream is sometimes stirred into the sauce when it is cool.

Madeira Sauce

Sous S Madyeroy

600ml (1 pint) basic red sauce
150ml (¼ pint) Madeira wine

25g (1oz) butter

Pour the wine into the sauce, bring it to the boil and add the butter. Stir until dissolved.

Serve hot with roast meats.

Red Wine Sauce

Sous Iz Krasnovo Vina

90ml (3fl oz) red wine
75g (3oz) sugar
1 teaspoon cornflour

1 strip lemon rind
Water

Pour the wine into the saucepan, add 90ml (3fl oz) of water and the rind. Bring to the boil. Mix the cornflour with a little water to a paste, stir this into the wine. Add the sugar and without taking the pan from the stove, stir the sauce until the sugar is dissolved.

Adjust the sugar according to taste and the quality of the wine, that given above is too much for my taste.

Serve with game meats, or mutton, or with sweet dishes.

White Wine Sauce for Fish

'Byeloye Vino' Sous

1 small parsnip
1 small onion
50g (2oz) butter
25g (1oz) plain flour
about 600ml (1 pint) strained
  fish stock

Salt and pepper
1 egg yolk
2 tablespoons dry white wine
Lemon juice to taste

Clean the parsnip and chop it finely. Peel and mince the onion. Melt half the butter, add the parsnip and onion, and simmer gently until soft. Blend in the flour and gradually pour in enough stock to make a sauce. Bring this to the boil, add salt and pepper and cook fairly rapidly for 7 to 10 minutes. Take the sauce from the heat. Beat the egg yolk into the remaining butter and stir this into the sauce. Rub through a sieve. Return to the pan, reheat, add the wine, stir, take the pan from the heat and add about 1 teaspoonful of lemon juice.

Test the fish stock before using, it may be seasoned enough, in which case no more salt or pepper will be required.

RUSSIAN cooking

Sour Cream Dressing I

Zapravka Iz Smyetany I

Mix in equal proportions sour cream and wine vinegar. Add salt, pepper and mustard to taste.

Sour Cream Dressing II

Zapravka Iz Smyetany II

Mix 150ml (1/4 pint) of sour cream to 1–1 1/2 tablespoons of wine vinegar. Add sugar to taste.

Sour Cream Dressing III

Zapravka Iz Smyetany III

Mash 2 egg yolks until smooth and beat into about 150ml (1/4 pint) of sour cream. Add salt and pepper to taste and whisk until the sauce is creamy. If this is a little too thick, dilute with a little fresh single cream or milk to the consistency required.

Mustard Dressing for Salads

Zapravka Gorchichnaya

2 teaspoons prepared English
  mustard
1/4 teaspoon each salt and pepper
3 teaspoons sugar
Vinegar, very little and
  preferably wine or tarragon

Lemon juice
Olive oil, or vegetable oil,
  enough to bring the
  dressing to a smooth
  consistency

Mix together the mustard, salt, pepper and sugar, then add the oil and when this is blended into the mixture and the sugar quite dissolved, add a little vinegar and lemon juice and, inally, enough oil to bring the mixture to the usual salad dressing consistency.

Leave for 30 minutes before using to allow the dressing to settle. Finely chopped fresh dill, chopped gherkins and parsley can also be added.

This dressing is meant primarily for use with cold meats, poultry, game and fish.

Table Mustard

Gorchitsa Stolovaya

English mustard powder
Hot water
Vinegar

Vegetable oil
Sugar and salt

Mix all these ingredients together (to taste) to the usual mustard consistency.

Or

1 teaspoon English mustard
  powder
1 teaspoon sugar

Tiny pinch salt
Boiling water

Mix these ingredients together with enough boiling water to make a smooth paste. The boiling water dissolves the sugar and gives a smoother texture to the mustard and takes away any bitterness.

RUSSIAN cooking

Jams
Varyeniye

Russian jams, which are excellent, are thicker and more solid than those usually prepared in Britain. The fruit is not pulped but preserved whole. This method of jam making improves the appearance of the jams, a matter of importance to the Russians since jam is not spread on bread, but is served in small glass dishes or saucers and eaten with a spoon, usually with tea. Quite a number of Russians like to take a spoonful of jam, put it into their mouths and then drink a sip of tea.

In the olden days, preserves and pickles were very necessary to Russian cooks for the long days of winter, when the earth offered little or nothing, and roads and railways were blocked. Judging by much of the Russian literature of pre-Soviet days most of the summer was spent by industrious cooks in preparing for the winter. An aroma of pickling spices, of mushrooms, cucumbers or cabbage filled the air as these important items of Russian diet were 'laid down'. Apples, pears, grapes and cherries, all were carefully pickled in their due season and from them a store of wonderful pickles and drinks were made. Vodka and brandy were great helps in general preserving, as indeed the latter was in earlier days in Britain. Many of the Russian preserving recipes are identical to those given in older cooking books in Britain.

When boiling jams, whether of the Russian variety or of the British, it is quite a good tip to smear the preserving pan well with butter first, to prevent the sugar from burning.

Apricot Jam

Varyen'ye Iz Abrikosov

900g (2lb) fresh apricots
900g (2lb) sifted sugar

600ml (1 pint) water
1 tablespoon lemon juice

The apricots should be fresh and ripe enough to break easily into halves. Rinse the fruit in cold water. Drain. Halve and stone (some recipes say peel).

Crack the stones, pick out the kernels and put these into a muslin bag. Put the apricots into a dish and cover with half the sugar. Leave for 24 hours.

Next day bring the remaining sugar and water to the boil. Add the fruit, with all the syrup which has oozed from it, the bag of kernels and the lemon juice. Shake the pan gently until the apricots are immersed. Cook over a low heat, gradually increasing it. Scrape off the foam as it rises. When the apricots become transparent the jam is ready. Remove the bag of kernels. Pour the jam into scalded jars, cover and seal immediately.

A tablespoon of vodka may be added just before the jam is ready.

Small apricots do not require halving and stoning. Simply prick them all over, pour boiling water over them and leave for 5 minutes. Drain. Rinse the apricots in cold water. Drain again. Immerse the apricots in a syrup prepared with the sugar and water and bring to a slow boil. Remove from the heat and leave for 40 minutes. Add lemon juice, bring again to the boil and cook until transparent.

Cherry Jam

Varyen'ye Iz Vishni

900g (2lb) Morello or black cherries   700g (1 1/2lb) sifted sugar
  (weight after stoning)   Water

Stone the cherries. Crush the stones and boil in a little water, this draws out their flavour and increases the flavour of the jam. Strain.

Put the sugar into a pan with this liquid, plus enough water to make 450ml (3/4 pint) of liquid. Cook this to a syrup, add the cherries and the lemon juice and cook slowly until the jam is so thick it will hardly drop from a spoon. Pour at once into scalded dry jars and seal immediately.

Other suggestions to improve the flavour of the jam are: soak the cherries in the syrup for 3 to 4 hours before cooking; or drop the cherries as you stone them into any liqueur before cooking.

Black or Morello cherries are usually used by the Russians in jam making, but other cherries may be used, provided they are ripe and firm.

RUSSIAN cooking

Cranberry Jam or Preserve

Varyen'ye Iz Klyukvy

900g (2lb) cranberries   125ml (4fl oz) water
1.8kg (4lb) sifted sugar

Clean the cranberries, remove the stalks and rinse several times in cold water. Pour the water into a pan and add alternate layers of cranberries and sugar. Boil gently and skim carefully, but do not take off the boil. After bringing the cranberries to the boil, continue to cook for another 10 minutes, or until they are soft. Pour into scalded jars and seal at once.

Cranberries are prolific in Russia.

Gooseberry Jam (Green)

Varyen'ye Iz Kryzhovnika

900g (2lb) gooseberries   Finely grated rind and juice 1 lemon
700g (1 1/2lb) sugar   450ml (3/4 pint) water

Top and tail the gooseberries. Soak in water for 6 to 8 hours. Put the fruit into a pan, bring slowly to the boil and let it boil until very soft, stirring and mashing frequently. Take the pan from the stove, gradually add the sugar and lemon, stirring until the sugar has dissolved, then return the pan to the heat and bring quickly to the boil. Simmer for 45 minutes. Test for setting. Pour into scalded jars and seal.

Green, under ripe gooseberries are considered the best for this particular jam.

Plum Jam I

Varyen'ye Iz Sliv I

900g (2lb) plums
1kg (2¼lb) sugar

Lemon rind and juice
300ml (½ pint) water

Slit the plums and take out the stones. Or, if preferred, simply gash them with a knife and skim off the stones as they rise to the top of the pan when cooking.

Spread out the plums on a baking sheet and sprinkle them with sugar. Leave overnight, or up to 24 hours. Next day put them into a preserving pan with the water and sugar and bring very gently to the boil, stirring with a wooden spoon to prevent burning. Carefully remove all the scum and, when no more appears, add a squeeze of lemon juice and a small piece of lemon rind. Bring the plums to the boil and cook quickly for 15 minutes. Pour into scalded jars and seal in the usual manner.

Crack a few of the stones, take out the kernels and add these a few minutes before taking from the pan.

Plum Jam II

Varyen'ye Iz Sliv II

2.7kg (6lb) plums
2.7kg (6lb) preserving sugar

300ml (½ pint) water

A few of the plums should be stoned and the kernels blanched. Put the water and sugar into a preserving pan and let this dissolve over a slow heat. Add the plums and take off the heat for the night.

Next day slowly bring to the boil, then cook quickly for 30 minutes, stirring all the time to prevent burning. Test to see if it sets, add the kernels and boil up once more. Pour into hot, dry scalded jars and seal at once.

Damsons can also be cooked in this way.

Both the above jams are very, very thick.

RUSSIAN cooking

Quince Jam

Varyen'ye Iz Aivy

900g (2lb) quinces
1.4kg (3lb) sugar

1.7 litres (3 pints) water
2 tablespoons lemon juice

Wash the quinces, and cut into slices. Pour half the water over the peels and cover and bring to the boil. Strain. Return the liquid to the pan, add the quinces, cover and cook gently until they are soft.

Pour off the liquid and mix this with the sugar and water, and cook to a syrup. Add the quinces, bring to the boil and add the lemon juice. Lower the heat and cook for 1 hour, stirring constantly, or until the jam becomes transparent and jelly easily. Pour into scalded jars and seal.

Rose Petal Jam

Varyen'ye Iz Lyepyestkov Roz

450g (1lb) rose petals
1.4kg (3lb) sugar

Juice 1/2 lemon
300ml (1/2 pint) water

Pluck the petals from pink and red roses when dry and fresh, white ones should not be used. Cut off from each petal the hard white base, which is bitter and makes the jam a bad colour. Cut up the petals finely and mix with 450g (1lb) of sugar. Leave them in the preserving pan overnight, or for a few hours. Make a syrup with the remaining sugar, lemon juice and water. Add the sugared rose petals and simmer until the jam jells, about 30 minutes, stirring almost all the time. When ready put into sterilized jars and cover.

The roses are best gathered while the dew is still upon them, and very carefully wiped. One English recipe I have suggested that rainwater should be used.

Jams
Varyeniye

Strawberry Jam *(Baltic-Russian)*

Varyen'ye Iz Klubniki

900g (2lb) strawberries
900g (2lb) sifted sugar

600ml (1 pint) water

Do not wash but roll the strawberries gently back and forth in a cloth. Sprinkle with sugar, not too much, and leave the strawberries for a few hours.

Cook the remaining sugar with the water and, when it begins to thicken, carefully add the berries. When they come to the boil, take the pan from the heat. When the boiling subsides, return the pan to the heat and bring again to the boil. Repeat this process 3 times. Cook the berries over a very low heat until the syrup is so thick the berries fall to the bottom of the pan, and the syrup hardly falls from the spoon. Pour into a glass container, leave covered until cool, then pour into jars.

RUSSIAN cooking

Preserves and Pickles
Marinady I Solyen'ya

Preserves and pickles are a necessity for the Russians during the long winter months but, even so, pickling and preserving are not the arts they were in former times. As elsewhere in the world, Russian cooks have lost their inclination to do their own pickling or preserving and prefer to buy commercial products when they can.

Usually such products are in any case cheaper, but nowhere are they as well-flavoured as home preserved or pickled products. The following recipes are not difficult. Some of the recipes are similar to our own British recipes, others distinctively Russian.

Ivan Goncharov in Oblomov gives an excellent description of a Russian storehouse in a middle-class or perhaps average bureaucrat's house in the last century.

'There were huge jars of coffee, cinnamon and vanilla, crystal tea caddies, cruets of oil and vinegar. Whole shelves were taken up with packets, bottles and boxes of household remedies, herbs, lotions, plasters, decoctions, camphor, fumigating powders; there was also soap, material for cleaning lace, taking out stains and so on ...

'In the store, hams, cheeses, loaves of sugar, dried fish, bags of dried mushrooms and nuts bought from pedlars, were strung up to the ceilings so that mice could not touch them. On the floor there were barrels of butter, big covered jars of sour cream, baskets of eggs and all sorts of good things. Another Homer would be needed to describe in full detail all that had been accumulated in the corners and shelves of this small ark of domesticity.'

Salted Beetroot

Svyekla Kvashyenaya

1.4kg (3lb) beetroot   1 tablespoon salt

Wash and peel the beetroots, grate and mix with salt. Pack into a wide-mouthed earthenware container. Cover with a wooden lid and keep this down with a weight. Leave for 15 days.

The liquid which comes from the beetroot can be used in flavouring borsh, or as a drink.

Pickled Beetroot

Svyekla Marinovannaya

1.8kg (4lb) beetroot   Salt

Marinade

600ml (1 pint) vinegar   2–3 cloves
Small piece of cinnamon   300ml (1/2 pint) water
Little grated horseradish   6 peppercorns
1 bay leaf

Wash the beetroots thoroughly, taking care not to damage the skins. Cook in boiling, salted water until tender, or until the skins are easily removed.

Put the marinade ingredients into a pan, bring to the boil, lower the heat and simmer for 5 minutes. Cool before using.

When the beetroots are cooked, drain, peel and cut them into fairly small cubes, or thick slices. Pack into a large glass, or earthenware jar as closely as possible. Strain the vinegar and pour this over them. Seal tightly and store in a cold place.

Beetroots, because of their high sugar content, ferment easily, so this type of pickle is best made in small quantities.

Instead of boiling the beetroots they can be baked at 190°C/375°F/Gas 5 for 1 1/2–2 hours. Although the recipe does not stipulate salt in the vinegar marinade, about 2 teaspoons is an improvement.

RUSSIAN cooking

Salted Cabbage (Sauerkraut)

Kapusta Kvashyenaya

1 very large white cabbage
50g (2oz) salt

12 peppercorns
1/2 teaspoon caraway seeds

Strip off all the outer leaves of the cabbage (keep these), cut it into 4 pieces and remove the thick stalks. Wash the cabbage, drain it and shred as finely as possible. Lay some of the whole cabbage leaves at the bottom of an earthenware jar, or small wooden cask, add some of the shredded cabbage, a layer of salt, some peppercorns and caraway seeds. Repeat until all the cabbage, salt, etc, has been used up. Cover the top with cabbage leaves, a clean piece of cloth and a wooden lid. On top of this put a weight.

Store in a fairly warm place. After fermentation begins, it will continue to ferment for 4 to 5 weeks. When this stops, the cabbage is ready for use.

During this process it is as well to change the top leaves from time to time.

To store the sauerkraut for a long time, put it in a cool but dry place. It should keep for months.

Marinated White Cabbage, Georgian Style

Kapusta Marinovannaya Po-gruzinski (Tbilisi)

1 large, firm white cabbage
1 chopped and cooked beetroot
4 tablespoons vinegar
Chilli pepper to taste

Chopped celery, fresh parsley or dill
 to taste
Enough boiling water to cover
 the cabbage

Strip off the outer leaves of the cabbage, cut it into 4 pieces and remove the thick stalks. Cut the cabbage (do not shred) into smaller pieces and put it together with the beetroot into a jar. Add celery, pepper, parsley or dill and enough water, mixed with the vinegar, to cover the cabbage. Keep in a warm place for 2 to 3 days.

Before serving, take out and discard the beetroot, parsley and celery, and arrange the cabbage in the 'form of a rose'. Serve cold with cold meats.

Red Cabbage Marinated

Kapusta Krasnokochannaya Marinovannaya

1 large red cabbage	*Marinade as for preceding recipe*

Strip off the damage leaves from the cabbage, cut it into 4 pieces and cut away the thick stalks. Shred the cabbage as finely as possible and wash it thoroughly. Prepare the marinade and let it cool. Pack the cabbage into a jar, or cask. Strain the marinade and pour this over the cabbage. Cover and store in a cool place.

Another recipe suggests putting the shredded cabbage into a bowl, sprinkling it generously with salt, and leaving it for 24 hours before packing it into jars and marinading.

Salted Cucumbers

Ogurtsy Solyennye

12 very small cucumbers	*6 peppercorns*
1.2 litres (2 pints) water	*Fresh dill and garlic*
4 tablespoons salt	*Mustard seed to taste*

Soak the cucumbers for 12 hours in cold water. Next day drain them and put into an earthenware jar. Mix the salt, water, peppercorns, dill, garlic and mustard seeds together, and pour this over the cucumbers. Cover the jar tightly, making quite certain the cucumbers are completely covered with water.

The cucumbers will be ready in a few days. If required quickly, cut off their tops before putting them in the jars. Salted in this manner, the cucumbers will not keep a very long time.

It is better to have the cucumbers all the same size when salting them, short, green, not too ripe, and not too chubby.

Grated horseradish, fennel, caraway seeds and vine or tarragon leaves are other flavourings used in salting cucumbers.

Failing small cucumbers, use the larger ones, peeled and cut down the centres from top to bottom, then cut each piece lengthways again, then cut into 5cm (2in) lengths.

RUSSIAN cooking

Salted Tomatoes

Tomaty Solyenyye

Tomatoes are salted in all their stages of development, ripe, half-ripe and under-ripe. They should be all of equal size. Best of all are garden fresh tomatoes.

5.4kg (12lb) tomatoes	1 long green pepper
5.7 litres (10 pints) water	Fresh dill or tarragon
450g (1lb) salt	

This recipe is for ripe and just under-ripe tomatoes. For green tomatoes add more salt and no herbs.

Dissolve the salt in the water. Place a layer of leaves at the bottom of a wooden cask, or earthenware jar. Add a layer of tomatoes, a sprinkling of herbs, more tomatoes and herbs until the cask or jar is filled. Pack as tightly as possible, filling the tub to the top. Add the salted water, it must cover the tomatoes, cover with a wooden lid, add a weight and leave for 6 weeks.

Possibly more tomatoes will go into the cask, so that the quantity of them given above can only be approximate.

Preserved Apples

Yabloki Mochyenyye

Cooking apples can be preserved in either of the following liquids, the quantity varying according to the number of apples, but it must come to at least 7.5cm (3in) above the apples. Blackcurrant, oak or cherry leaves should line the bottom of a tub, or stone jar, as well as to put between the layers of apples.

No. 1 Liquid

9 litres (16 pints) water   3 tablespoons salt
450g (1lb) sugar

Bring this to the boil and leave to cool before pouring into the jars.

No. 2 Liquid

200g (7oz) rye flour   10.2 litres (18 pints) water
2 tablespoons salt

Bring the water to the boil, take the pan from the heat, stir in the salt and rye flour and leave for a while. Then strain and pour into the jars.

Put the apples into a barrel or jar, alternating them with layers of the leaves. The apples should be stalk upwards or, as the Russians say, 'Apple legs upwards'. Cover with remaining leaves. Keep the apples for the first few days in a temperature of 15°C/60°F. After that the temperature may be increased. The apples will be ready in 40 to 50 days.

Instead of lining the barrel with leaves, it can be sprinkled with rye or wheat flour. When the level of the liquid falls, add more water.

RUSSIAN cooking

Pickled Cherries

Vishnya Marinovannaya

900g (2lb) black cherries, preferably Morello

Marinade

300ml (1/2 pint) wine vinegar
600ml (1 pint) water
350g (12oz) sugar
2.5cm (1in) piece cinnamon

2–3 cloves
Pinch cayenne pepper
Small piece root ginger

Wipe the cherries carefully, and take off the stalks. Put into an earthenware or glass jar.

Put the marinade ingredients into a pan and bring to the boil. Simmer for 5 minutes and leave until cold. Cover the cherries and seal down tightly.

They will be ready for use in about 4 weeks.

Pickled Grapes

Vinograd Marinovannyi

Take the grapes from the stalks and put into a deep jar with wine vinegar to cover. Seal and store in a cool place. They will be ready in 1 month.

Or make a marinade as for pickled cherries (see recipe above) using half as much sugar and no ginger. Pour this marinade over the grapes when cold, seal and store. They will be ready in about 4 weeks.

Pickled grapes are particularly good served with chicken or with fish, and with boiled ham.

Uncooked Fruit Preserve

Pyurye Iz Svyezhikh Yagod

This method of preserving fruit, it is claimed, retains about 70 per cent of the vitamin C in fruit and is best suited for the berry type of fruit. It can be used as a filling for pies, tarts and cakes, etc, and also for fruit sauces.

225g (8oz) mashed fruit   225g (8oz) sugar

Wash the fruit thoroughly in cold water, turn out on to a dry, absorbent cloth, then drop into an earthenware bowl and mash. Add the sugar. Return the fruit to the bowl and leave in a cold place for 6 hours. From time to time stir thoroughly. Pour into sterilized jars and store in a cool, dark place.

Apple Spread

Povidlo Iz Yablok

Apples, as required
Sugar, as required

For each 225g (8oz) of apple purée use 75g (3oz) of sugar.
   Cook the apples until very soft and rub through a sieve. Measure and return the purée to the saucepan. Add the sugar and cook the mixture slowly until it thickens. Take the pan from the heat, pack into hot, sterilized jars and cover immediately.
   Use as a spread on bread or in any of the ways in which jam is used.

Plum Spread

Povidlo Iz Sliv

For each 225g (8oz) of plum pulp use 100g (4oz) of caster sugar.
   Rinse as many plums as required, stone and put into a pan without adding any water. (If the plums are not sufficiently juicy, add just enough water to prevent burning. Drain this off before rubbing the plums through a sieve.) Cook the plums slowly until very soft and, while still hot, rub through a sieve. Measure and return this pulp to the pan and cook until the mixture is fairly dry. Add the sugar and continue cooking until the mixture is thick. Pack into sterilized jars and seal in the usual manner.
   The above recipe can be varied slightly and turned as follows into a sweetmeat suitable for storing.

RUSSIAN cooking

After returning the plum purée to the pan (having carefully measured it), add icing sugar instead of castor sugar, in the required quantity, and continue slow cooking until the mixture leaves the sides of the pan. While still hot spread this out on a flat dish or baking sheet and leave in the sun for 3 days or in a simmering oven for 12 hours. When the paste is very dry, cut into shapes and roll in caster sugar. Pack into glass jars with sheets of paper between each layer. Sprinkle the top with castor sugar before sealing.

Such sweetmeats are usually cut into fancy shapes, such as diamonds or triangles. A similar and excellent sweetmeat recipe comes from Uzbek.

900g (2lb) mixed fruit (apples,
cherries, prunes or apricots)
700g (1½lb) icing sugar

50–75g (2–3oz) ground almonds
2 beaten egg whites
Vanilla flavouring (optional)

Prepare the fruit, it is not necessary to peel or core the apples or even to stone the fruit, since it is to be sieved. Cook all the fruit in very little water until soft, and rub while still hot through a sieve. Return to the pan, add the almonds, sugar and vanilla and cook until the mixture thickens and is quite dry. Add the egg whites, beating the mixture until the whites are completely blended into it. Spread over a tin or greased baking sheet and leave in a very slow oven (140°C/275°F/Gas 1) to dry and become firm. This process takes several hours and it is one of drying out rather than baking. When set, cut into fancy shapes or slices and leave until cold. Store as in previous recipe. Can be served with afternoon tea or as an after dinner dessert.

In this recipe the prunes and apricots are better not soaked. If the mixture is too 'wet' it will not dry out and will become simply a spread. Instead of ground almonds, walnuts may be used, or a mixture of both. I have also added sultanas and figs to the mixture.

Beverages
Napitki

By and large Russian beverages are much the same as in our own country. Tea is the staple drink, although the average Briton would not consider what the Russians call tea as being tea.

Coffee is extremely popular, but not much to the foreigner's taste, except perhaps what they call 'Eastern' coffee, which is what we call Turkish. There are also several coffee drinks well-laced with alcohol.

Among the soft drinks there are some fruit juices, of varying flavours and qualities. Almond-flavoured milk drinks rate high; so do milk shakes of all descriptions. Ice-cream is good, even Americans agree on this point, and it is sold on the streets of Moscow (and elsewhere) not only in the summer but throughout the bitterly cold winter days. I suppose one cannot get any colder. Ice-cream sodas are extremely popular.

Russian beer is more the Continental type of beer and inclined to fall flat. Kumys and kvas are both fermented drinks and popular throughout the country. This latter drink has several varieties and is usually fermented with black bread. And there is a good kvas fermented from apples. Kefir, which comes under drinks, is a Russian type of yoghurt.

Formerly Russia was a paradise for schnapps drinkers, but vodka was and still is the national drink. In the old days vodka, which was indiscriminately distilled from a variety of grains (also potatoes), was often as high as 100 per cent proof. Today it is a less fiery product altogether. The best vodka, some Russians declare, is as low as 30 per cent proof, and in any case is good for the general health, which of course takes the glamour and the sting out of vodka.

Contrary to general belief vodka is not always a clear, liquid. There are several varieties. There is the favourite, lemon vodka; there is 'English vodka' with a slightly bitter flavour; there is a pepper vodka, and a Jewish vodka; there is a herbal vodka, and there are those flavoured with Morello cherries, apricot or blackcurrant leaves. Apart from this there is a red and yellow vodka, and those which are 'improved' upon with, for example, an infusion of cornflowers which turns the liquid a soft blue, or mint which both colours and flavours the vodka, or saffron which gives it a rich amber colour.

The correct way in which to serve vodka is in tiny glasses which can be

RUSSIAN cooking

emptied in one gulp. This procedure is not as startling as it might sound, since the 'swallows' are small. Just throw the head back and hope for the best, was the advice given to me. Then eat something. Vodka, according to the Russians, should never be taken without eating, therefore it is served with the *zakuski* and, indeed, throughout a meal, except, naturally, with the sweet course. To drink vodka without eating, insist the Russians, is bad for the stomach.

In some parts of Russia there is a curious custom of a young man proving himself before his friends, when he falls in love. This consists of the girl's first name being spelt out on a table in glasses of vodka, the contents of each of which he must swallow. For the man who loves his Anastassiya the ordeal must be quite something, or perhaps it hardly matters after the first six letters have been downed. What happens if the young man fails this test, which is to prove him a man, I am not quite sure; my informant only giggled when asked.

Apart from drinking vodka or testing one's manhood, there are other more prosaic uses for it. Cooks declare that a tablespoon or so in a chocolate cake mixture makes the cake lighter. Another use is to mix it with tooth powder and use as a silver polish, while beauticians say 'fill a bottle with quince seeds, add vodka to cover, and leave for a long time'. From this operation results a thick syrup which can be used as a hand lotion and skin softener. It is true, I have found, about the chocolate cake, but the other two suggestions I have not tried.

Wines are rather too expensive for the average Russian. Opinions vary considerably as to the quality of Russian wines, but generally they are considered inferior to French wines of all kinds. Some declare that although these wines are pleasant to drink they leave an unpleasant aftermath and nasty taste in the mouth. Another, who has had more experience than I of grapes, told me he considered Russians 'brutalized' their grapes. 'There can be no hope for their wines.'

At the time of writing, the old Massandra Winery of the Tsars in the Crimea is still in existence, now state-run, and produces a wine tasting attraction to tourists in this area. The grapes, grown on the shores of the Black Sea, are made into wine for sale in the government stores. it is a fascinating place, with deep underground tunnels, seven in all, in which are stored thousands of bottles of wine. Many of these are of recent vintage, others aged from two to five years are in barrels. There is a 'museum piece' of Spanish wine of 1775 vintage, and the racks also hold wines which are a couple of hundred years old, taken from the Tsars' cellars. The Tsar's seal is still on them but the contents have probably long ago turned to the sourest vinegar. Visiting tourists are usually offered a glass of wine from the winery which produces some 15,000 barrels of wine annually.

Russian wines do not have names such as Medoc or Beaujolais. They are numbered in the most unromantic manner possible. You can get a red wine 'No 41' from Georgia, which is considered quite good. But however pleasant it may taste, it loses much of its glamour with this dull numbering. Quite often, when ordering wines in a restaurant, it is discovered that due to some jolly bit of bureaucracy one restaurant has all the white wines and another the red.

'Champagne,' Stalin is reported to have said, 'is a sign of a nation's prosperity.' I know Americans who have taken the trouble to ship Russian 'champagne' back home, but I was unable to discover whether it was because it would be a curiosity or whether the Russian champagne is really better than the American produced variety. In any case it falls far below the French quality. It is palatable, to say the least.

Again there is a fair variety of liqueurs, vodka being the basis of all of them. Brandies and cognacs are in the Russian champagne class, although again there are those who praise them highly. I suppose it is all in the taste buds.

Home-made Vodka

We have Russian friends who make vodka in the bath. I have not tried this, although I have quite often drunk theirs without ill effect. My recipe is for a more sober quantity, and can be made in quantities to suit the individual.

Mix some pure alcohol with boiled water to dilute it, a little more water than alcohol makes the vodka 45 per cent proof. Add a knob of sugar and a very thin strip of lemon rind. Remove this latter before serving. Keep for 12 hours.

An old recipe suggests that for ladies a somewhat 'lighter' drink is usually preferred and therefore the lemon rind is omitted and hot red wine added instead. This latter vodka should be 35 per cent proof and must be allowed to cool for at least 24 hours.

One is supposed to judge for oneself just how much hot red wine is required.

RUSSIAN cooking

Apricot Vodka

This has much the flavour of the Hungarian barack or brandy.

1 litre (1³/4 pints) pure alcohol   450g (1lb) sugar
750ml (1¹/4 pints) water   450g (1lb) apricots

Make a syrup with 600ml (1 pint) of water and all the sugar. While this is cooking, halve the apricots, smash the kernels, and add all this to the sugar syrup. Bring to the boil, take from the heat, and let it stand overnight. The next day strain the syrup into a large bottle, add the alcohol and remaining water, stir well and cork. Keep for 3 months.

The fruit can be used for making jam, marmalade or apricot fool, or simply with cream as a dessert.

Tea

Chay

Tea is the universal Russian drink. But not tea as we know it. Russian tea is usually made on a samovar. The samovar contains lighted charcoal from which fumes escape up a vertical central flue. Round this heated centre is a container of water which is drawn off from a small tap. On the top is a decorative openwork stand on which rests the china pot in which the tea extract, or essence, is kept heated and the tea stewed.

The tea is served in tall glasses, in the best homes in silver containers, with no milk, but plenty of sugar, or jam, and thin slices of lemon are added. The Russians like jam with their tea and in the country (in some cities, too) many people like to put a spoonful of jam in their mouths and drink through it. Or they will use a knob of sugar, or a boiled sweet.

The tea in the little pot is very strong; 2 heaped teaspoons of black tea, over which is poured 450ml (³/4 pint) of boiling water. It is steeped for 5 minutes, then a little of the infusion is poured into each glass, and the glasses are then filled from the water in the samovar.

Samovars in these days are plain, without frills, and are electric, working on the percolator principle. Antique samovars are in great demand and a really good one fetches a high price.

Although charcoal is the usual fuel for heating the samovar, wood, or pine cones are also popular, as the cones are sweet smelling.

The word 'samovar' means, more or less, 'to boil by itself'. A very old-fashioned Russian remedy for colds was to put blackcurrant jam, or other jam which had plenty of vitamin A, into the tea before adding the water.

Tea, Kirghizian Style

Atkanchay

600ml (1 pint) milk
1 heaped teaspoon black tea
25g (1oz) butter

125ml (4fl oz) sour cream
Salt to taste

Brew a very little strong tea, add the milk, and bring to the boil. Strain, return to the pan, add the butter, salt and sour cream and bring again to the boil.

Serve hot in small porcelain bowls with rolls or buns previously cut into halves and fried in hot butter.

Dunking is permitted.

I have not tried this recipe since I don't like tea flavoured with milk and sugar. Adding butter and sour cream would only add, as far as I am concerned, to its unpleasantness. However, I offer the recipe to the curious and add that it has a resemblance to some tea I was once made to drink in a Tibetan-Nepalese monastery, there the butter was rancid. I did not like it at all.

Tea with Red Wine

Chays S Krasnym Vinom

125ml (4fl oz) weak tea
90ml (3fl oz) red wine
Sugar to taste

Pinch cinnamon
Pinch ground cloves

Heat the wine, add the cinnamon and cloves and simmer for 2 to 3 minutes. Pour this into a glass of tea, without adding milk but with sugar to taste.

RUSSIAN cooking

Fermented Liquid

Kvas

This is used both as a drink and as a basis for some Russian soups.

There are several ways in which one can make kvas and Russian cooks used to make their own. But times have changed and today in Russia long queues of shoppers can be seen buying kvas at the shops.

900g (2lb) black rye bread
6.8 litres (12 pints) boiling water
600ml (1 pint) sugar-syrup, or
    black treacle

25g (1oz) yeast
1 tablespoon plain flour
50g (2oz) raisins
2 teaspoons lemon juice

Slice the bread and, either lightly toast it, or let it become dry in the oven. Put the slices into a large earthenware jar, cover with boiling water and leave until the water is tepid. Strain. Mix the yeast with the flour and stir into the strained liquid. Add the syrup, or treacle and stir until it is thoroughly blended into the liquid. Leave to ferment for several hours, at least 12, or until the foam begins to settle on top of the kvas. Strain again and then pour into bottles, adding 2 or 3 raisins to each bottle. Cork very tightly and tie the corks down with string. It is important to seal the bottles tightly, otherwise they are likely to explode. Store the bottles in a cool place, lying down. The kvas will be ready for use in a few days. Kvas has been described sometimes as a type of light beer.

Beetroot Kvas for Borsh

450g (1lb) raw beetroots
1.2 litres (2 pints) water, boiled
    and allowed to become tepid

1 thick slice rye bread, the
    darker the better

Wipe the beetroots, peel thinly, chop, or slice and put into a jar. Add the water and the bread, cover loosely with a cloth, and leave the jar in a warm place for 3 to 4 days.

This kvas is meant only for borshch and not as a drink.

If rye bread is not available coarse brown bread also makes a passable kvas.

Sour Beet Kvas

A Jewish Passover sour beetroot kvas for making borsh, to be served during Passover.

Scrub as many beetroots as required and remove the tops. Cut into halves, or quarters and pack into an earthenware crock, or pickling jar. Fill to at least 5cm (2in) above the beets with boiled water which has been cooled to lukewarm. Cover and leave for 3 to 4 weeks, or until the mixture has become sour.

Fermented Mare's Milk

Kumys

This is a cultured, sweet and sour, fermented drink made from the milk of mares, asses and camels. It used to be fermented in horsehide bags and maybe such drinks are still fermented in this manner in some of the more remote parts of Russia where it is still a popular beverage.

It is mildly alcoholic, containing, however, only 1 to 2 per cent alcohol, and the more strongly and more often the kumys is stirred with a long stick, the better it is said to be. It is a rather thin liquid, drunk throughout the country by Russians but not so much by foreigners, although I have known those who profess to like it.

The origin of kumys is pre-Christian. Both Pliny and Xenophon have written of its merits, both declaring that kumys tasted best of all when the bag containing it was carried on the back of a wildly bucking horse. Marco Polo compared it to an excellent white wine.

As a drink kumys was made famous by the Kalmuck Tartars, brewed by them from a mixture of mare's and camel's milk. And it was drunk by Genghis Khan himself. According to Marco Polo, the great Khan maintained a stable of about ten thousand white horses, all as white as snow, and only the direct descendants of the Khan were allowed to drink milk from the white mares.

Despite its low alcoholic content, Russians are apt to regard kumys as a highly intoxicating drink.

At one time in America a type of kumys was readily available in drug stores, but prepared from cow's milk which doubtless would have made a Tartar weep had he known of this. With the advent of yoghurt the sale of

RUSSIAN cooking

kumys in the States went out of fashion. Unless the right culture is used it is not possible to prepare the drink at home. And outside of Russia the right culture is as hard to come by as the kumys itself.

'Travelling' Drink *(or One For The Road)*

Napitok 'Dorozhnyi'

125ml (4fl oz) red wine
50ml (2fl oz) dry white wine
sugar to taste

Nastoyka, a type of flavoured
cognac (lemon, tangerine
or cherry). Add to taste

Mix the red and white wines, add sugar and the flavoured brandy and bring to the boil. Serve hot.

Sportsman's Drink

Napitok 'Sportivnyi'

150ml (1/4 pint) red wine
Sugar to taste
Water

Lemon or tangerine rind to taste
Cloves and nutmeg, also to taste
Pinch cinnamon

Cook the sugar in a little water until it dissolves, add the wine, cinnamon, cloves, nutmeg and rind. Bring to the boil, strain and add a fresh piece of peel as a garnish when serving.

Cranberry Juice Drink

Napitok Iz Klyukvyennogo

Cook the berries until soft, rub through a sieve, dilute with water and add sugar to taste.

This particular drink is recommended as not only being very refreshing but also as an antidote against sweating. Instead of water, fizzy or soda water may be used.

RUSSIAN cooking

Index

RUSSIAN cooking

Index

RUSSIAN cooking